Submarine

The USS *Pickerel* bursts from the deep. The 48° angle was deliberate; there is no record of the effect on the submarine's crockery.

Overleaf HMS *Resolution*.

Submarine

Jonathan Crane

BRITISH BROADCASTING CORPORATION

Acknowledgements

The Submarine Service has traditionally been the most secretive branch of the Royal Navy, and I am grateful to them for allowing that policy to be partially modified for the sake of a television series.

In particular, I would like to thank Commander Barry Coward, whose patience and positive help I much appreciated during filming; Commander Dai Evans, who, despite the tremendous pressures of running Perisher, was unfailingly helpful, courteous and, above all, fun; Commander Jonathan Cooke, who did everything in his power to smooth the path of filming; Commander Mike Hawke and his wife Juliet, for their generous hospitality; and Michael Hill, overworked Public Relations Officer to the Submarine Service. I would also like to thank the members of the Perisher course 2/83, and the crews of HMS *Oracle*, *Warspite* and *Repulse*.

Published by the
British Broadcasting Corporation
35 Marylebone High Street
London W1M 4AA

First published 1984
Reprinted 1985
© Jonathan Crane and
the British Broadcasting Corporation 1984

ISBN 0 563 20326 9

Typeset by Phoenix Photosetting, Chatham

Printed and bound in Great Britain by
Mackays of Chatham, Limited

Contents

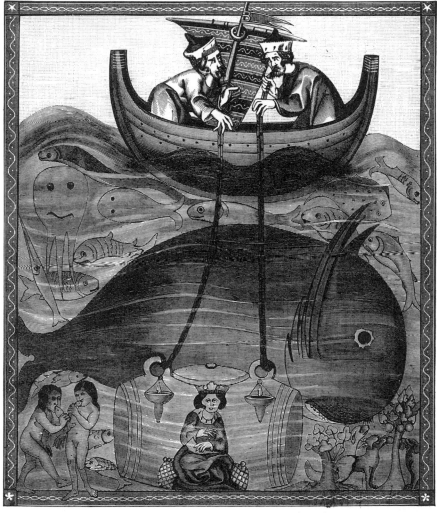

The first (probably apocryphal) attempt at a submersible craft: Alexander the Great's descent into the Bosphorus in 332 BC. (*See page 107.*)

Picture credits

Introduction

The battered blue Navy bus swings round and stops on Campbeltown pier. Twenty-five submariners and I climb reluctantly out, wincing at the kind of raw, wet gale that only the remote west coast of Scotland can produce.

Unpainted and unprotected against the spray, the fishing smack *Mary MacLean* noses out of the bay, feeling her way through the appalling weather. The grey sea and the grey clouds merge into an indistinguishable horizon – visibility could be fifty yards or 5000. The submariners crowd together in the stuffy, windowless cabin, in limbo but already at ease.

'*Mary MacLean*, *Mary MacLean*, this is *Warspite*, this is *Warspite*, do you read me?' A rendezvous point is arranged; the skipper offers a prize for the first sighting. Trained eyes scan an utterly empty sea.

'There she is – on the port bow.'

A hump-backed shape, dark and silent, wallowing gently in the swell. The rounded lines of the hull, with the sleek fin on its back, have none of the proud bearing of the frigate or destroyer. This is menacing, mean, mysterious. The *Mary MacLean* bumps alongside; we clamber up a rope ladder on to a narrow, slippery-wet deck and are unceremoniously bundled down a small, round hatch.

Suddenly it's warm and dry and bright. Everyone is in shirt-sleeves, officers in crisp white shirts. Many of the crew wear open-toed sandals, some without socks. Tea in the wardroom is served in white china, with saucers and silver spoons; chintz-covered chairs, watercolours on wood-panelled walls, Beethoven on the concealed stereo system. Cupboards display silver birds and pewter tankards; a steward puts biscuits on the green baize table.

'May I have details of your next of kin?'

A submarine is a totally controlled, well-ordered world in which you can almost forget what is outside. Almost, but not quite.

The nuclear-powered submarine is a formidable machine. It is the capital ship of the navies of Great Britain, America, France, Russia and the People's Republic of China, the only five countries to possess it. To the newcomer, though, it is a long, crowded metal tube that is about to take him down into the chilly depths of the North Atlantic.

A submarine diving is impressive when seen from the surface. Columns of spray shoot twenty feet high as water rushes into the space between the boat's internal and external hulls and forces the air out. The submarine soon starts to settle deeper into the water, the foreplanes angle downwards and bite into the waves, and within minutes the periscope has disappeared. It is a strange experience to look at a piece of completely undisturbed water only thirty yards away and know that just a few feet beneath the surface is 285 feet of black submarine, absolutely invisible, but exuding a threatening and almost tangible presence.

Inside the submarine diving is an anticlimax. In the packed control room, no one shouts 'Dive, dive, dive'. Just 'Open main vents', and a few switches are flicked. 'Six down, keep 120 feet' sounds better, but six degrees of bow-down angle turns out to be barely enough to feel. The periscope is lowered, the depth gauge inches round, but there is no change of noise, no creaking hull, no trickling leaks. The truth is that it feels the same whether the submarine is on the surface or at 500 feet, at five knots or twenty-five. The only difference is in rough weather. A nuclear submarine is shaped to travel fast underwater, and its rounded hull makes it relatively unstable on the surface, where it rolls in heavy seas. There is a submarine saying: 'Happiness is 500 feet in a force 10 gale.'

It is not only comfort that makes submariners prefer to be dived. They feel uneasy on the surface, and vulnerable to detection. Submariners pride themselves on their invisibility, and even in coastal waters a submarine will 'transit' from one port to another dived, however unimportant detection may be at that particular time. There is a feeling of relief when the submarine dives; oblivious to the outside world, it falls gratefully into a familiar routine of watchkeeping, sleeping and eating. Sliding silently through the cold water, the submarine is now in its natural environment.

Right HMS *Warspite.*

CHAPTER 1
Ocean Safari

Her Majesty's Submarine *Warspite* is one of the Royal Navy's thirteen nuclear-powered hunter-killer submarines. It displaces 4500 tons (more than a frigate), draws thirty feet when on the surface (more than the aircraft carrier *Hermes*), and has a complement of 110 men (three times the crew of a World War II U-boat). Its nuclear reactor will drive it at over twenty miles per hour on the surface, and considerably faster under the water. Its depth gauge stops at 1000 feet. There are two electrolysers which provide unlimited air to breathe, distillers which provide unlimited fresh water, and nuclear fuel which needs replacing every five to six years. The only limits to endurance are food and the mental stability of the crew. *Warspite* recently completed the longest continuous patrol ever by a Royal Navy submarine – 112 days. The submarine did not need to surface for the entire period.

The hunter-killer's job in peacetime is to contact, follow and analyse Russian submarines. Its job in wartime would be to sink them. To this end it has ultra-sensitive equipment that will pick up the

sound of another ship many miles away, and sixteen 22-foot-long torpedoes that are guided, yard by yard, to their target.

Personal space on *Warspite* is minimal. The Captain has the luxury of his own cabin, measuring about six foot square, into which is crammed a bunk, which doubles as a seat, a desk, a wash-basin and a small clothes-cupboard. The four most senior officers share two cabins, the remaining eight share one about the size of a small kitchen. Bunk space for them is almost identical to that enjoyed by the ratings: six feet long, two feet wide, a one-foot gap between the mattress and the bunk above, with curtains to pull to cut yourself off. Storage space is one small locker about two foot by one foot by one foot which must contain uniform, boots, books and personal effects for up to three months.

Bunk space for the ratings is in two lumps of forty bunks each, squeezed into an area the size of the average garage. Visitors and trainees enjoy the mixed blessing of sleeping in the 'fore-ends'. Right up in the bows, the fore-ends contain the torpedoes and their firing tubes. The upper section is used for storing spare torpedoes in wartime only; in peacetime it's the accommodation overflow.

A nylon sleeping bag and pillow, rolled up on a thin red mattress. My bunk. Two others alongside, so close that they touch, all slung on racks four feet from the floor. Beneath, three more bunks lie parallel; to the left, across a narrow passageway, six more laid out identically; behind, another twelve. In front, torpedo-firing equipment. Beneath the floor, visible through the open grating, sleek, black torpedoes wait to be rammed into their firing tubes. The whole compartment almost seems designed to remind the nervous newcomer of what he's let himself in for. The fore-ends double as an escape compartment; a watertight bulkhead separates the rest of the submarine. There is an escape hatch and emergency breathing apparatus and red-painted safety equipment everywhere. To escape, water must first be flooded in up to chin level, to balance the internal and external pressures.

Climbing into my bunk requires extreme contortions to avoid pipes and lockers. Turning over is just possible; the hull is only one foot above my face. Lying on the mattress I can hear a faint trickling, a reminder of the tons of water pressing against the hull. An occasional drip – of condensation – should be the straw that breaks the camel's back. And yet I feel no anxiety.

Despite the popular myth, claustrophobia is just not a problem amongst submariners or even their visitors. Perhaps this should not be too surprising; after all, a London tube-train or a passenger aircraft are similar in scale, and most people use them quite unconcernedly. It is the potential danger of the submarine's

HMS *Trafalgar*, one of the latest nuclear-powered Fleet submarines.

environment that is the basis of the expectation of claustrophobia; but since the potential claustrophobic is completely unaware of that environment, he is unlikely to be worried by it. Apart from one startled awakening in the early hours of the morning, when the submarine's sonar equipment produced an extraordinary rippling sound which seemed to run right around the outside of the hull, I experienced no worries whatsoever about diving. I even tried quite deliberately to induce such a feeling, as a test of my subconscious, but there was no latent fear there whatsoever.

There are many surprising domestic details in a submarine which also help the newcomer to forget what is outside – although many of them are just a little different because it is a submarine. Food comes three times a day at normal mealtimes, and there is a reasonable choice. For the first few days at sea salads appear frequently, but thereafter, as the cooks dig deeper into the massive deep-freeze, fresh foods gradually disappear. For the last weeks of *Warspite*'s record-breaking South Atlantic patrol the crew were reduced to a diet of tinned tomatoes and mince. There is a tiny shop for cigarettes and chocolate, crammed into an impossibly small office up a ladder. Beer is available, and the senior ratings' mess even has a proper bar where pints are pulled. Spirits are forbidden whilst at sea, and officers will only admit to an occasional glass of wine with their meal. Ratings are theoretically limited to two pints of beer a day.

On any nuclear-powered submarine so much spare fresh water is distilled for the engineering systems that there is always plenty for washing and showering, although shaving aerosols, like paint, glue and boot-polish, are forbidden: the gases could contaminate the endlessly recirculated atmosphere. Films are shown most evenings, but have to be switched off when there is the danger of detection and the submarine goes to its 'quiet state'. Day and night are separated by a change in the lighting. At sunset, the control room and wardroom will switch to dim red lights, to accustom periscope-watchkeepers' eyes to the gloom outside. Although many of the crew must keep watch during the night, a submarine is a quieter place in the small hours of the morning. Sleep tends to be in short bursts; six hours on, six hours off is the pattern for most of the crew. Although the body rapidly adjusts, it is not surprising that this is the subject where submarine slang is at its most eloquent; a submariner will proudly announce that he is off to his scratcher/cart/pit/rack to get his swede down/do some Egyptian PT/ rack out/count deckhead rivets/carry out an eyelid inspection/crack in a few Zs.

At the end of my first day on *Warspite*, I already felt an involved part of what was a very real world, but one which existed in a kind of limbo; we could have been anywhere, at any depth. In fact we were travelling south, towards the Azores, where we were to take on the role of a Soviet submarine and spend the next ten days testing the defences of a major group of NATO warships.

Ocean Safari is an annual NATO exercise, held in the Eastern Atlantic, designed to test participating countries' defences against attack by Soviet warships. Any conflict in Europe would rapidly lead to the need for massive convoys shipping supplies from the USA – just as in World War II. And, as in that war, the principal threat to those convoys would come from submarines. It is a major exercise, with ninety warships and a token force of eighteen ships representing unarmed merchant ships. Despite the depletion of the Royal Navy's available submarine force as a result of patrols in the South Atlantic, the Chief of Naval Staff considered the June 1983 Ocean Safari sufficiently important to withdraw *Warspite* from another less significant exercise for these two weeks. *Warspite* herself had in fact recently returned from the South Atlantic, and, after a brief stay in port, most of the crew were glad to have the prospect of some action. Falklands patrols are one of submariners' least favourite tasks: two weeks of fast transit to the south, followed by up to ten weeks of uneventful patrolling, followed by another two weeks of fast transit back, is nobody's idea of fun.

For the exercise, *Warspite* was to take on the role of Soviet Charlie- and Victor-class submarines. Its job was to attack the convoys and 'sink' as many ships as possible. Although no real torpedoes were to be fired, a complex set of rules dictated that the submarine would have to manoeuvre relatively close to its target before simulating firing, and could then retreat to reload with more theoretical torpedoes before returning to the fray. One officer casually referred to the exercise as 'a turkey shoot', implying that it would be all too easy. His prediction, as it turned out, was not altogether true.

Much of the exercise would be spent testing the practice of the new defended-lane convoy theory. Traditionally, a group of anti-submarine warships have escorted a convoy of merchantmen, shepherding them from port to port. The major disadvantage of this method is that the speed of the convoy is limited by its slowest member. If a merchant ship should break down, difficult decisions are faced by the escorts as to whether to wait for it or leave it to fend for itself. The defended-lane theory creates a clearly-defined strip of water to the north and south of which patrolling escorts search for intruding submarines, allowing the merchantmen to travel at their own speed inside the protected seaway. Long-range sonars enable the escorts to be relatively widely spaced; the question is whether the benefit of allowing the merchant ships freedom and flexibility to proceed singly and at their own pace is outweighed by the comparatively thin defences of the lane at any one point.

Ocean Safari was due to start on Wednesday, 8 June. On 5 June *Warspite* dived in the Irish Sea, still several hundred miles from where the exercise would happen, for what the Captain hoped would be the last time for two weeks. However, minutes after diving we already had a problem. The outer casing, or hull, of a submarine is carefully designed and constructed to create as little disturbance – and therefore noise – as possible underwater. Smooth, rounded lines, reminiscent of a dolphin's shape . . . flush-fitting bolts and screws to fasten down hatches . . . retractable bollards for use only in port . . . close-fitting steel shutters that snap shut over the bridge when the submarine dives. Any noise the submarine produces both reveals its position to the enemy and makes it deaf by clogging up its own sensors. Imagine then the sonar operators' reaction when, shortly after diving, they start to set up and test their equipment, only to be deafened by a loud and persistent knocking from outside the submarine.

The captain is called. He tries changing speed and depth, but it makes no difference. 'Noise is extremely important to us – or the lack of it. It is particularly important in this major exercise, as the way we'll be detected is by the noise signature that we produce. The rattle itself is quite a serious one, it's noisy and it's one we didn't have before. It will be a serious disadvantage to us in that it makes us deaf in detecting other ships and it makes us more detectable by potential enemies. So we're going to surface again immediately to see where the rattle is – there's no external threat to us now and the weather is good – both may change by tomorrow.'

But this was not *Warspite*'s day. Even surfacing proved difficult. A submarine underwater has neutral buoyancy; in theory it will ride naturally at any depth, with no inclination to rise or fall. Any depth changes are achieved entirely by using the hydroplanes, the equivalent of an aircraft's flaps. To surface, positive buoyancy is gained by forcing the water out of the area between the inner and outer skin of the submarine by injecting air at high pressure. This air is stored in tanks and is precious. Knowing that he would not have the opportunity to replenish these tanks for some time, the Captain decided to surface using what's called the 'blower'. In this method, only a small amount of air from the high-pressure tanks is used; then the blower sucks air out of the internal hull of the submarine itself to displace the last few gallons of water needed to bring the submarine fully to the surface. The blower's powerful fans cause a small drop in air pressure inside the submarine which makes ears pop, and the process takes a little longer, but it does conserve that precious high-pressure air.

However, any submarine that has been in port for a few days has minor faults, and *Warspite* was no exception. The blower had already given trouble during routine system-testing, and should by now have been fixed. But, much to the Captain's chagrin, his order 'Start the blower' did not lead to the expected hum of fans and rush of air; only to a sharp reproach to a junior engineering officer who was unfortunate enough to be held responsible for the blower. A few minutes later the fans whirred into action, we surfaced, and the knock was traced to a piece of loose equipment underneath the torpedo-loading hatch near the bows of the submarine.

Soon we had dived again and were moving south, fast and silent. *Warspite* by now had settled into its normal seagoing routine. The control room is the nerve-centre. It is right in the middle of the submarine, directly beneath the fin (which is what ignorant newcomers call the conning tower), with the engine room behind and living accommodation in front. The size of a large kitchen, the control room is packed with equipment and, for much of the time, with people too.

On the right-hand side are all the controls needed to manoeuvre the submarine in any direction. A panel of switches and valves controls the flooding and venting of the buoyancy tanks and, just as important, adjusts the trim of the submarine. Neutral buoyancy is achieved by having just the right amount of water in all the different tanks that run the length of the submarine. Too much water in the bow tanks will give the submarine a nose-down angle, and a tendency constantly to go deeper; too much in the stern tanks, and it will always be pointing to the surface. After a spell in port, when equipment and stores have been moved around all over the submarine, it takes the Officer of the Watch some time to achieve level trim by pumping water from one end of the submarine to the other. The final adjustments are really quite small; perhaps fifty gallons of water, weighing less than a quarter of a ton, will make all the difference to 4500 tons of submarine.

To the left of the trim panel sit the two planesmen. Strapped into their seats, handling what looks exactly like a joystick and staring intently at a massive array of dials and instruments, the planesmen look more like pilots than sailors. The analogy is not, in fact, so inaccurate. *Warspite* has two sets of hydroplanes – movable horizontal control surfaces on the exterior of the hull – which control the attitude and depth of the submarine, much like an aircraft's wing-flaps and tailplane. On a submarine, the forward planes control the depth of the submarine and the after planes the angle; the two functions are obviously linked, and changing depth requires both operators to use a delicate touch. They are effectively 'flying' the submarine and, just like an aircraft, it must be gently handled. It is possible to execute quite violent manoeuvres, both horizontal and vertical. Sharp turns, where the submarine heels *into* the turn (unlike a surface ship which leans out), can produce 45° of heel – and in an emergency depth change the submarine can point 20° downwards. It is for this reason that the planesmen are strapped into their seats, and the Officer of the Watch behind them stands in what is called the 'bandstand' – a waist-high circular support which he can hang on to when the angles become extreme. Everyone else in the control room must either hang on tight to the nearest pipe or handle, or they must keep their balance by deliberately leaning into the angle; the latter looks more nautical, but seems curiously out of place in an environment so divorced from the natural elements.

The left-hand side of the control room is dedicated to pinpointing other shipping, and if necessary destroying it. Charts, screens and displays showing a wealth of information, much of it highly classified, are packed tightly together. Side by side at the centre of

HMS *Valiant*, another of *Warspite*'s sister submarines.

the control room, dominating it, are the two periscopes. Weighing 1¼ tons each, these fifty-foot-long steel cylinders of complex optics are the real epicentre of the submarine. At periscope depth they can be raised or lowered hydraulically in seconds, and are the Captain's eyes; but when raised above the surface they are the most detectable part of the submarine. So the periscope is invaluable – but it can also be the submarine's downfall.

The bigger of the two, the search periscope, has an upper head about six inches across, with two sets of lenses sending an excellent image down to the control room. But a six-inch-wide piece of glass and steel travelling at six knots provides an all-too-clear wake, and an image on radar too; so for all close-in work the attack periscope is used. Its head has only one lens, and is a mere two inches across. The image is not so good, but quite acceptable.

Unlike the bridge of a ship, which is visited only by the men who work there, the control room of a submarine is also a passageway for anyone else who needs to pass from the sound room, wardroom or officers' accommodation to the rest of the submarine. This makes

The Valiant class *Warspite* is capable of over 20 knots on the surface, particularly when 'on the step', as seen here. A sharp turn at full speed pulls the bow up on to its own bow-wave; the stern drops, and the submarine is planing.

HMS *Warspite* is one of the Royal Navy's thirteen nuclear-powered Fleet submarines. First commissioned in 1967, it displaces 4500 tons, has a complement of 110 men and six torpedo tubes.

Overleaf Warspite at maximum speed, approaching Ailsa Craig.

Warspite diving. The plumes of water from the main vents can be clearly seen by the foreplanes. It takes about five minutes for a Fleet submarine to dive; with a submarine that spends 90% of its time underwater, there is no need for the traditional rapid crash dive.

On *Warspite*'s cramped bridge. The navigator and his look-out demonstrate the submariner's penchant for idiosyncratic clothing.

Commander Jonathan Cooke on *Warspite*'s bridge, returning to Plymouth from the NATO exercise 'Ocean Safari'.

A Sub-Harpoon submarine-launched anti-ship missile. Fired from a torpedo tube by submarines such as *Warspite*, it has a range of about 20 miles.

HMS *Churchill*, *Warspite*'s sister submarine.

HMS *Sovereign*, a Fleet submarine of the Swiftsure class. Built in the 1970s, this class has many classified improvements in sonar and electronic capabilities. Externally it is similar to the Valiant class, except for the position of the foreplanes, which are below the waterline.

The *Warspite* wardroom. At the head of the table is the First Lieutenant, Lt Cdr David White; on his right is the Captain, Cdr Jonathan Cooke.

The senior ratings' mess on HMS *Warspite*.

it less remote, more informal than a ship's bridge; it could be one of the reasons for the informality between officers and men that is a feature of submarines.

Directly aft from the control room is the reactor tunnel, beneath which lies the nuclear core of the submarine. It is never touched during patrol, and the fuel needs changing only every five to six years. This is one of the major costs of a submarine refit; a hole must be cut in the deck to allow the spent fuel container to be lifted away and replaced. Beyond the reactor tunnel lies an engineer's dream – a myriad of turbines, pumps, generators, control panels and, ultimately, a single shaft that silently turns the massive propeller. This pocket nuclear power-station produces enough electricity to power a large town.

The whole concept of taking a miniaturised nuclear power-station to sea, throwing it around at violent angles from the surface to several hundred feet down, and expecting it to work perfectly, is somewhat audacious. To be responsible for all or part of that feat must create a sense of pride amongst the 'back-afties'; but with many of them that pride is deeply buried beneath the engineer's traditional grumbling exterior. True, much of the engine room is not a comfortable place in which to work. Nuclear-powered or not, *Warspite* is steam turbine-driven, and that means heat and humidity. True, the reactor cannot be shut down and forgotten in a few moments, unlike the rest of the equipment on board, which makes short port visits no holiday for the engineer. True, no engineer can ever show his wife where he works; the engine room is a strictly prohibited area to most visitors, especially potentially pregnant women. But lurking quietly behind the grumbles is usually a grudging admiration for the machinery and a quiet feeling of indispensability; after all, the submarine can survive without radio, sonar, sophisticated navigational aids and so on – but without power it is lost. It is not surprising that one third of the ship's complement and nearly half its length are devoted to keeping it alive.

Opposite the reactor tunnel are stairs which lead down to a long passageway which runs almost to the bows of the submarine. Leading off it are accommodation areas, senior and junior ratings' messes, the galley, the coxswain's office and, down more stairs, the 'heads' – showers and lavatories, also separated for senior and junior ratings. The major accommodation space is effectively a rectangle with three tiers of bunks either side of a continuous passageway. There is just enough room to slide into the bunk, turn over and stretch out. There are curtains which, when drawn, provide the only privacy a submariner can have. A tiny locker houses his personal belongings; most clothes have to be stored under the mattress. A few photographs, an occasional reminder of home such as a cuddly toy, and as often as not a personal stereo set, are the limits of the submariners' private world whilst on patrol.

Moving further forward, a single galley provides for all 110 men. It is directly beneath the wardroom (with a dumb waiter sending up the food) and in between the senior and junior ratings' messes. The senior ratings' mess looks much like a small lounge bar in an average English _pub. At one end, in fact, is the bar, behind which a reproduction oil painting of a submarine hangs on the wall. Spare barrels of beer, topped with cushions, double as seats. A video-recorder, TV set and film projector are the principal sources of entertainment. Mealtimes are crowded, and there is no time to linger over dessert; your place will be needed for the next sitting. The junior ratings' mess is similar but more spartan; no attractive wall lights, no tasteful oil paintings.

Moving even further forward, the 'fore-ends' are usually the quietest place on the submarine – except during a firing or simulated firing of a torpedo, when they become a cacophony of hissing air, rushing water and shouted orders.

The 'heads' are gleaming stainless steel, rigorously cleaned every day. Each mess has its own group of six basins, three lavatories and a shower; tucked in between is the laundry, which provides an efficient overnight service.

On Monday 6 June, at 1200 hours, all officers (except those needed on watch in the control room and engine room) and several key senior ratings file into the tiny wardroom. Twenty people in all, tucked into every corner, with the latecomers – and ratings – having to stand. There is an expectant buzz of conversation. Finally the Captain makes his entrance, beautifully timed just one minute late.

'We're all assembled for the operations brief for Ocean Safari, which starts the day after tomorrow. This is a major NATO exercise, so we must make every effort to play it as for real . . .'

Commander Jonathan Cooke is looking forward to Ocean Safari. Like the rest of his crew, he found the Falklands patrol tedious and is hoping for plenty of activity in the next two weeks. Forty years old, laconic and somewhat languid in his manner, Cooke has a reputation for aggressive tactics as a submarine captain. This command will be his last before going ashore to 'drive a desk', in Navy slang.

'In a NATO exercise, just to remind you, there are two sides; Blue forces, simulating the NATO alliance, and Orange, who simulate the Soviets. In this case we're going to be the Soviets, or Orange, which is good – it's always more fun playing the baddies. So we will be simulating a Russian submarine throughout the exercise, and simulating Russian systems for which they are credited. I'll now pass you over to the First Lieutenant who will give you the details.'

The First Lieutenant, Cooke's second-in-command, is Lieutenant Commander David White. This is White's first post as First Lieutenant on a nuclear submarine, and he is keen to make his mark. Fully charged with nervous energy, talkative and a strict disciplinarian, 29-year-old White is the perfect foil to his Captain, who patiently tolerates his subordinate's desire for maximum efficiency throughout the submarine.

White's briefing starts with this old Etonian sheepishly stating 'Orange's' version of the political background that has brought the two sides to the verge of war – or at least to the verge of Ocean Safari.

'Breakdown of relations between Blue and Orange has been caused by Blue propaganda and accusations over Orange involvement in Blue politics. Blue's increase in military expenditure has caused us to prepare for the defence of our homeland. This has been misinterpreted by Blue who has placed its forces on high alert. Our aim as Orange is to shadow these forces and then to strike the first blow by pre-emptive attack on Wednesday.'

The news about the submarine's programme for Ocean Safari is taken to the senior and junior ratings' messes by their Presidents. Leading Seaman Gordon King is President of the junior ratings' mess, and he has a hard time getting everyone's attention; they are in the middle of eating lunch. He struggles to relay the information against a barrage of noisy indifference and finally loses all credibility when he accidentally mispronounces the name of one of the French warships, the *Foch*. Submariners, like any sailor, will never publicly display enthusiasm about their operational programme – they maintain a convincing façade of grumbling disinterest, complaining that it is all a waste of time and that exercises such as Ocean Safari simply mean extra work. Whilst this is probably true for some of them, the reality is that many were grateful for the opportunity of some action, however simulated it was going to be – but they were determined not to show it.

One of the many preparations for Ocean Safari is to perfect the ship-recognition techniques of any officer who may be on periscope duty. Despite the unofficial motto of the service, 'There are only two kinds of ships, submarines and targets,' it is essential that he should be able to recognise the class, nationality and type of any ship that may be involved in the exercise, so that it can immediately be identified as friend or foe. However, he will get only a brief and distant view through the periscope, so lengthy slide sessions are arranged every day. David White flashes often-blurred photographs up on the screen for a few brief seconds, before asking an officer to identify the ship. There are warships from several different NATO countries – British and Dutch frigates, American destroyers, Canadian oilers, even a French aircraft carrier. Also interspersed are Russian warships and submarines, who may well take a close interest in the exercise. Every conceivable opportunity is used to display the shapes of the ships; photographs are plastered all over the control room, and every day a rating dutifully changes the four that can be squeezed on to the wall of the officers' lavatories.

Meanwhile *Warspite* is moving quietly into warmer water as we approach the Azores. The temperature inside the submarine is slowly rising, and the atmosphere is becoming humid. For one morning we are accompanied by a school of dolphins; their complex conversations are clearly audible on the sonar loudspeakers – an infinite variety of squeaking, screeching and whistling sounds that defy interpretation. Shortly afterwards a continuous rattling sound on the same set reveals that we are passing through a shoal of shrimps.

On Tuesday, 7 June at midday, the Navigator, Lieutenant David Cooke, does a final confirmation on our position, cross-checking the submarine's own inertial guidance system with the satellite navigation read-out and his own dead-reckoning estimates, puts down his pencil on the chart of the eastern Atlantic, and walks down the short passageway from the control room to the Captain's cabin.

'Captain, sir, we're in the start position for Ocean Safari. I'm still steering 180° at eighteen knots. Our next course is 328° at twelve knots, so I'd like to slow down and come round.'

'Right, slow down, come round to the north-west, start the standard sonar search, and start the turbo-driven feed pumps so that we're in immediate readiness for full-power state. Brief the ship's company that the exercise has begun, and that although war has not yet broken out, we're in a period of rising tension, and that all Blue forces can be regarded as hostile, whether surface warships, submarines or aircraft. Remind everyone about keeping the noise down.'

On the way back to the control room, David Cooke puts his head round the door of the sound room to alert them to listen hard for any contact. Just fifteen minutes later they announce a warship contact. It is reported to the Captain who takes the precaution of closing up the attack teams. But after further investigation, it transpires that the warship is in fact tens or even hundreds of miles away, and its sound emissions have reached us only through freak underwater conditions.

Warspite's first prearranged engagement will in fact signal the outbreak of hostilities. It is to be a combined attack on the French aircraft carrier *Foch*, which will be attacked simultaneously by the American submarine USS *Gato*. Although this attack is still twenty-four hours away, *Warspite* is now fully on the alert for any Blue forces; from now on it is essential to remain invisible and undetected. In the sound room, sonar operators listen intently to every noise; the periscope is continuously manned by the officer of the watch.

But on the morning of 8 June, before the exercise has even fully started, the submarine is detected. The Captain has just finished a short stint on the periscope and handed over to Russ Cameron, the ship's Supply Officer, who raises the periscope, takes one 'all-round look', and immediately snaps the handles up and orders it to be lowered again. 'There's a white flare just two cables away,' he reports to the Captain. Cooke moves back to the periscope, checks for himself, and confirms Cameron's sighting. He also spots an Atlantique, a French anti-submarine detection aircraft, flying a short distance away.

The Atlantique must have been using the aircraft's standard technique of submarine detection, which is to dip a small sonobuoy into the water, which picks up radiated noise from any nearby submarine. The pilot has dropped a flare to show that he has made contact with the submarine. Cooke immediately orders the submarine to 400 feet and comforts himself with the hope that it may be a 'friendly' aircraft.

'One of the problems with an exercise such as Ocean Safari is that you don't always know whether an aircraft like that is on your side or not; both Blue and Orange forces have Atlantiques. The probability, though, is that it belongs to the Blue forces. It's embarrassing, because it means he's localised us, so I'm moving away from the area as fast as possible. At least "war" hasn't yet broken out, so it's not as bad as it might be.'

Still, it is a bad start to Ocean Safari; the position of the submarine is now known to the Blue forces, which must weaken the chances of carrying out an unhindered attack on the *Foch*. Worse is yet to come.

The *Foch* attack will not use torpedoes, but a weapon called Sub-Harpoon, which looks like a torpedo and indeed is fired from a torpedo tube, but subsequently behaves quite differently. Instead of rushing through the water towards its target a few thousand yards away, Sub-Harpoon behaves more like an Exocet missile. Shortly after firing it bursts through the surface, skims low over the water, and homes in on its target tens of miles away – well beyond visual range. *Warspite* is relying on intelligence about the position of the *Foch* and its protecting escorts from the Maritime Headquarters at Pitreavie Castle, just outside Dunfermline. Pitreavie receives information from other ships, aircraft and satellites and will in turn control the general deployment of Blue forces. So far the intelligence Cooke has received from there is not sufficiently fresh to give him a reliable idea as to where the *Foch* is, so he can't even move to within sonar-detection range. The attack must happen at 6 pm on 8 June; unless both *Warspite* and the USS *Gato* have sufficient information to be sure of co-ordinating their attack, and indeed to be sure of attacking the right force, they cannot fire.

At 12.30 pm the submarine is again at periscope depth. The sound room reports a faint contact; it could be the French task group. The First Lieutenant is on watch in the control room. He immediately reports the contact to the Captain in his cabin and they decide to go deep again, sprint at twenty knots towards the source of the noise, and quietly return to periscope depth to have a look.

The huge advantage any nuclear-powered submarine has over its diesel-electric counterpart is the ability to travel fast underwater. By matching or exceeding the speed of surface ships it can run rings around them, popping up in unexpected places to keep on attacking by surprise. However, at periscope depth the submarine must stay at slow speed – perhaps five or six knots – to avoid too obvious a wake from the periscope, and indeed to avoid damage to the periscope from the increasing pressure of water as it moves faster through the water. So the standard technique for submarines like *Warspite* is to creep slowly along, just beneath the surface, quietly watching the enemy, and then to lower the periscope, dive to about 400 feet and sprint at twenty to thirty knots towards their prey. If they simply remain at the shallow periscope depth the surface of the water will be disturbed by 4500 tons of submarine travelling at thirty knots; moreover, they won't be able to use the ocean's built-in cover.

As a submarine dives, it passes through water that becomes colder – and more or less saline. These changes in temperature and salinity produce what submariners call the 'layer', a swathe of ocean that bends sonar waves in strange directions and distorts the information that any anti-submarine escort receives. This layer can ultimately send the radiated sound waves from a surface ship back up to the surface many miles away, and it provides an invisible shield under which a submarine can hide. In addition, since the density and the depth of the layer varies, the task of analysing the distorted sonar information received becomes even more difficult for the surface ship.

HMS *Turbulent*.

It is this layer that allows *Warspite* to risk travelling fast and therefore produce more noise. Of course, the submarine's own speed and accompanying noise make its own sonar sensors useless – there is so much rushing water around the hull that any sonar contact is immediately lost. Thus, whilst sprinting at 400 feet the submarine may be reasonably safe but it is also deaf and blind, with no information about its prey from periscope or sonar. So, after its short sprint, the submarine must first slow down and allow the sonar operators to re-establish their contacts, and check that there isn't a ship directly overhead before nosing slowly and silently back to periscope depth

Twenty minutes later the periscope goes up; but there is nothing in sight. Cooke raises the wireless mast in the hope of intelligence signals from Pitreavie, but there is nothing of value. There is a growing feeling that the French have moved too far away to be attacked in the next few hours. The Captain is getting worried.

'There are just five hours left until we're due to launch this attack on the French task group. I still have only a general idea as to where it is and I need to be much more accurate than that, so I am becoming anxious for more accurate information, either from my own sensors or from the Orange surface task group or their aircraft on reconnaissance. If I don't get information from my own sensors or on the communications broadcast from the shore I may be forced to call up the surface task group, using a frequency that is detectable by all stations and which could therefore give my position away.'

At 4.30 pm we try to contact Pitreavie by satellite, but without success. Now there is a task group on the sonar screen which is known to be Orange forces; it is possible that they are themselves tracking the French. Cooke decides to go deep and sprint towards them – but thirty minutes later we slow down, return to periscope depth, and there is still nothing in sight. Neither are there any useful signals from Pitreavie. By now the control room is becoming resigned to the attack failing – as is Cooke.

'The news is no news – we have no further information on the force. The only ships we hold are down to the south-west, which we believe to be the UK task group who are not our targets. The chance of making an attack at the predetermined time in a few minutes is small. At this stage, even if we get the information, we'd be quite pushed to set up the attack, discharge the weapons and co-ordinate with USS *Gato*. So we'll just have to hope they're more successful, and we will merely live to fight another day. It certainly shows the difficulty of co-ordinated attacks.'

'So it's not been a very good day for *Warspite*?'

'It could have been better – there will be better days ahead though.'

An officer interrupts to pass a report from the wireless room. The Captain glances at it briefly. 'Right, that was again a negative result after calling our own task group. Wherever anybody is, they're not where we are.'

At 5.55 pm we've given up hope. But then, out of the blue, a signal arrives not from Pitreavie but from the USS *Gato*, giving a rough position of the French carrier. The entire control room is galvanised into movement: the submarine is correctly positioned to fire Sub-Harpoon; down in the fore-ends the missile-loading procedure is rapidly simulated. The information from *Gato* is fed into a computer in the control room, and the Captain gives the order to fire at 6.15 pm. It is a hasty business, and probably not as sure of success as it would have been with better information. There is even the possibility that the wrong target was attacked, but at least it is better than the anticlimax of not attacking at all.

We transmit a signal to Pitreavie giving details of the attack, and then as quickly as possible dive to a safe depth and sprint away from the scene of the crime. No escort pursues us; as far as we can tell no detection of any kind has been made.

The Captain switches on the main broadcasting system. 'Just a few words on what's been happening on the exercise front. We have just carried out a simulated Sub-Harpoon attack on the French task group, attacking the aircraft carrier *Foch*. That was a pre-emptive strike, as we've had the satisfactory role of being the baddies in this exercise. That means that "war" has now broken out, and that any future opposition we come into contact with we will be attacking. That is all.'

'Yes, I'm reasonably pleased with the attack. It could have gone better, it was a bit untidy, but as we say in the military, the aim was achieved.'

Is he certain that he hit the right target? In the rush to attack, could it even have been one of his own forces' ships?

'No, it would not have been one of our own ships. I can't guarantee it wouldn't have been one of the other ships in the *Foch* group. One of the problems with attacking a group of ships with missiles is the danger of them hitting the wrong one, but since the *Foch* is the biggest ship, the probability is that it's the one that was hit.'

With the attack over, *Warspite* now faces a day of fast transit to its next engagement, which is to locate and attack enemy convoys. The submarine falls back into its standard watchkeeping routine and a normal evening follows.

First Lieutenant's rounds is a daily ritual that David White enjoys with brisk enthusiasm. The coxswain, the submarine's senior rating, knocks on the wardroom door, cap in one hand and notebook in the other, to announce that *Warspite* is ready for inspection. White ceremonially puts his cap on too, and leads the way along the corridor. Using his torch to inspect every nook and cranny, he spends the next twenty minutes searching the entire submarine for untidy cupboards, dirty floors and any sloppily stowed equipment. Nervous junior ratings have been cleaning lavatories, scrubbing floors and tidying the areas for which they are responsible, knowing that the new First Lieutenant's eagle eye for detail will seek out any imperfection. The coxswain shouts: 'Stand by for the First Lieutenant's rounds,' as the two of them approach each new area, whereupon the ratings jump to attention and gabble their reports. Tonight, after climbing up and down ladders, poking under bunks, peering behind bulky pieces of equipment and even looking inside the galley's ovens, White can only find an untidy coil of rope with frayed ends to complain about. He disturbs the junior ratings who are in the middle of watching a film, by giving them a résumé of the day's activity; as soon as he leaves someone thankfully tells the projectionist to run the film again. White signs the coxswain's inspection log and another daily routine is over.

Around the submarine, as the evening wears on, other less formal rituals are unfolding. In the fore-ends, squeezed in amongst the torpedoes and Sub-Harpoons, a cook systematically pounds away on the exercise bicycle, engrossed in his book, *Iron Warriors of the Deep*.

A steward forces himself to an extra five press-ups. Another rating hangs up some washing on a makeshift clothes-line. The 'shop' opens, and ratings line up to buy chocolate and cigarettes. In the senior ratings' mess an argument is raging about which film to show. *Warspite* has taken several dozen films to sea on this trip, most of them recent releases. But tonight there is a vociferous lobby for the senior ratings' all-time favourite, the raunchy *National Lampoon's Animal House*. It has been run so often that they know most of the dialogue by heart, but tonight it is rejected in favour of an American film about a rebellion in a US army officer training school. A Chief Petty Officer laces up the projector, latecomers squeeze in between their colleagues to find a space on the floor, the lights go out and the titles roll. In the junior ratings' mess they've no doubts about what to watch: *Animal House* continues after the First Lieutenant's interruption.

In the wardroom, dinner is nearly over and the stewards are serving savouries, rather than sweet; they pride themselves on this particular custom, seldom serving the same one twice. The Captain glances at the three dials, set into the wood panelling, which display the submarine's speed, depth and heading. The conversation is mostly shop-talk, laced with jargon. Like all the services, submariners seem to initialise or abbreviate everything, from pieces of equipment to job descriptions and ranks. Thus the Weapons Engineer Officer is called the WEO, pronounced 'Weeyo'. If there isn't an abbreviation a nickname will do; so the Navigator is known as Vasco.

In the control room, pools of dim red light illuminate patches of equipment and faces; the rest is gloomy darkness. The control room goes to red lighting conditions at sunset, and remains in this fiery twilight for the rest of the night. Intent faces, many now sprouting embryo beards, catch a little extra red light from the instruments and screens that ring the control room. With the day's action over, desultory conversations float around this ghostly limbo. The ship-control officer of the watch, leaning against the bandstand, quietly explains the intricacies of trimming the submarine to a trainee rating. In front of him, the two planesmen stay silent as they concentrate on keeping the submarine precisely on depth . . . the navigator plots the submarine's course and checks its position against the display from the satellite navigation system. The watchkeepers on the fire-control side of the darkened control room are chatting idly about their last visit to Portsmouth, officer and rating both talking together as equals.

There's a tiny spare space just between the entrance to the reactor tunnel and the control room. Known by everyone on *Warspite* as 'grumpy corner', it is where hot and sweating engineers can take five minutes' break to smoke a cigarette and 'spin some dits'. A dit is submarine slang for a ditty, or story, or just an in-joke . . . and grumpy corner is where the dit-book is written, a very unofficial log of who is doing what in the submarine. Everyone's foibles, physical or of character, are mercilessly lampooned. In grumpy corner tonight, even in the midst of the laughs, jokes and endless comings and goings, a rating sits on the floor, knees hunched, intently reading a textbook, learning for his next examination. There is no privacy on a submarine.

The next two days pass without incident. *Warspite* continues on its fast, deep passage towards its next engagement, which will be the first in a series of attacks on Blue's convoys.

At 8.00 am on 11 June, the submarine comes alive with the call of 'Action Stations'. The brusque call on the crackly internal broadcasting system produces a variety of responses round the submarine. Men drop whatever they are doing, leave half-eaten breakfasts, tumble out of their bunks, and rush to their positions. The control room and sound room fill with people until there is barely room to move.

Two frigates, part of the forces defending the convoy, have been sighted. Strictly speaking, *Warspite* should be concentrating on attacking merchant ships, which are the important targets, but Cooke decides to have a go at the escorts. He spends twenty minutes slowly manoeuvring the submarine into an attacking position, but soon sights the convoy in the distance and immediately switches to attacking them. Torpedo attacks, despite the sophistication of the wire-guided Tigerfish torpedoes that *Warspite* carries, and which the Russians can match, still use similar techniques to those of forty years ago. Cooke must manoeuvre the submarine so that it is beam on to the merchant ship, to give the maximum width of target, whilst at the same time keeping an eye on all other vessels in the vicinity to ensure that there is no risk of collision. Although he has several computerised devices to help these calculations, it is remarkable how absolutely central a submarine captain is to every detail of an attack. He is the only person looking through the periscope – constantly taking ranges and bearings, calling out information about what he can see, assimilating data from sonar and the fire-control team. It is a marked contrast to operations on the bridge of a surface warship, where a whole team of watchkeepers can see what is going on, and where the captain will tend to give general orders and allow his team to execute the details.

The periscope is now hissing up and down every few seconds as we close to within a few thousand yards of our unsuspecting target, an unidentified tanker of 30,000 tons. Cooke must only raise the periscope when it is absolutely necessary; leaving it up constantly would greatly increase the danger of detection. At last we are in the right position; Cooke takes one final bearing and, with relish and gusto, shouts 'Fire'. The submarine shudders as compressed air shoots a slug of water from the torpedo tubes, simulating the real thing.

Control of the torpedo immediately passes to a rating on the fire-control desk, under the guidance of the Weapons Officer. He carefully guides the simulated torpedo, displayed on a screen in front of him, towards its target. A few minutes later the moving dot merges with the almost stationary dot of the tanker; we have scored a hit. In a real war, of course, the resulting explosion would alert the escorts to the presence of a submarine. So, to simulate this, Cooke gives the order for a green flare to be fired from the submarine; this is the standard method in exercises such as this of telling the world of a completed attack.

The flare arcs up into the sky and, depending on how alert the frigates are, will immediately give them our precise position. Without waiting to see what the reaction is, Cooke dives the submarine rapidly to 420 feet, and then slows down to allow the sound room to listen in. The sonar operators quickly provide a picture of what's happening on the surface. Sonar information, to the untrained ear, sounds like an incomprehensible jumble of clatters, whooshes, pings and rattles. But when skilfully analysed it provides the speed, type and direction of surface ships, what the weather is like, and whether they've found the submarine or not with their sonars.

The jigsaw of information rapidly fits together. Two distinct propeller noises are heard on different bearings – so there must be two ships up there. The rapid clatter of their screw noise betrays them as warships; merchant ships have large, slow-moving propellers that produce a low-frequency thump. There is a rhythmic fading and rising of the sound level of each warship; it must be bad weather, with the ships' sterns lifting out of the water in heavy seas. That would explain why they are only travelling at thirteen or fourteen knots, which has been deduced from their propeller speeds of about 108 rpm. Analysis of how many shafts each warship has, and even how many blades their propellers have, completes the identification of precisely which ships they are; this is confirmed by analysis of the sonar pings that are now bouncing off the submarine.

The final piece of the jigsaw is perhaps the most crucial; the sonar pings are becoming less frequent and fainter; neither warship has locked on to the submarine. Four hundred and twenty feet of ocean, with its changes in temperature and salinity, are protecting *Warspite* as effectively as a thick steel sheet.

However, all could change within moments; the escorts will not give up easily. What they do not know is whether *Warspite* will run away or return for another bite at the cherry – because there are several other merchant ships in the convoy. The morning turns into a game of cat and mouse between the hurrying escorts and the silent submarine.

Cooke decides on the bold manoeuvre of heading back into the lions' den – he slips back underneath the convoy and comes up on the other side for another attack. He considers it is what the escorts will least expect him to do; and anyway the propeller noise of the heavy merchant ships will disguise his own noise. We increase speed and soon can hear the heavy thumping of the tankers overhead; but there is no increase in the noise of the escorts. We seem to have shaken them off. *Warspite*'s manoeuvre is a classic example of the advantages a fast nuclear-powered submarine has over a conventional diesel submarine.

HMS *Sceptre* receives extra personnel at sea. Note the earthing pole carried by the rating on the right. The two men by the fin may soon need the helicopter's assistance.

Warspite reaches the other side of the convoy and prepares to return to periscope depth. In many ways this is the most difficult of all manoeuvres for any submarine. It is relatively easy to use the sonar to pinpoint all moving vessels on the surface, and to position the submarine so that it does not come up too close to them for safety; but that depends on the ships making some kind of noise. So the bane of a submarine captain's life are fishing boats and yachts. A fishing boat, when stopped and fishing, not only makes no noise but has large nets that spread hundreds of yards behind it. None of this registers on sonar, so there are regular incidents with submarines getting caught in nets, or occasionally even striking a fishing boat with their periscope as they come up to periscope depth. One such case happened in the Irish Sea when a submarine rose to periscope depth, became entangled in a fishing boat's nets, did not realise what had happened, and simply continued on its way, pulling the fishing boat behind it. Another Royal Navy submarine came up to periscope depth in the Channel and struck a fishing boat. The submarine's periscope and part of its fin were lost, and the captain now has a job ashore.

So, as *Warspite*'s depth gauge slowly winds round towards seventy feet, the control room is quiet save for the planesman calling out the depth and a rating manning a close-range sonar calling out any contacts. As the submarine passes through ninety feet, the Captain calls out, 'Raise attack,' and the attack periscope hisses up. Even though its head is still beneath the surface, Cooke swings the periscope back and forth to check that there are no unexpected dark shapes in the water. As soon as it breaks he does a rapid 360° 'all-round look'. There is nothing in sight; the rating on the close-range sonar takes off his headset, and the control room relaxes.

Cooke identifies the merchant ships in the convoy, which have started to zigzag; they are clearly expecting more trouble. The escorts are still on the far side, so we start to position for further attacks. In the next forty minutes *Warspite* slices through the convoy. At 10.04 we attack an unidentified bulk carrier of 20,000 tons; at 10.06 the motor vessel *Mercandian*, 4300 tons; at 10.10 the motor vessel *Seatrain*; and at 10.24 the Dutch warship *Zuiderkruis*. It is a maelstrom of activity in the control room, with the Captain taking ranges and bearings non-stop, and shouting 'Fire' every few minutes.

Inevitably our activity is spotted, and two escorts race towards us. Cooke has one final attack on the motor vessel *Gothia*, 2000 tons, getting close enough to get a full-frame photograph through the periscope before going deep and evading the escorts. They soon find us on sonar – we can clearly hear the pings from their sets.

For the next half-hour Cooke treats his submarine like an aerobatic aircraft. Twisting and turning, diving sharply to 450 feet and then back up again to 180 feet, alternately sprinting and crawling, he does his best to shake off his pursuers. He knows that the captain of one of the frigates is an ex-submariner, and it becomes a personal duel between them. The frigate holds on tenaciously, using her commanding officer's valuable underwater experience. *Warspite*'s control room concentrates single-mindedly on the reports from the sound room, waiting for the bearings of the frigates to change, indicating that they've moved away, and hoping that the intensity of the sonar signals will fade. Eventually they do; the two shepherds have returned to their decimated flock. *Warspite* relaxes once more and heads for the next patrol area where, according to the 'rules' of Ocean Safari, we will have reloaded with weapons from a Soviet supply ship and will be ready once more to attack a convoy.

We arrive at our new patrol area in the early hours of Sunday 12 June. Whilst looking for the convoy we come across two escorts, HMS *Brazen* and the Belgian frigate *Westhinder*. Cooke acknowledges that they are probably decoys, aiming to draw any enemy submarine's attention away from the convoy they are protecting; but again he cannot resist the temptation to attack, and 'sinks' both escorts. Now the absurdity of exercises such as these becomes clear: the 'sunk' escorts, alerted by our green grenade, start to chase the submarine. However, once more *Warspite* evades their attention and sprints off to search for the convoy; but they are nowhere to be found.

The action may be over outside the submarine, but inside it is still Sunday morning, and certain rituals must be observed. Breakfast on the Sabbath is distinguished by including 'seggies' (tinned grapefruit segments) and 'mushies' (tinned mushrooms), both of which are pounced on with squeals of delight, in the wardroom at least, and devoured as if they were gastronomic extravaganzas. Later in the morning, after the destruction of the escorts, comes Church. It is the Captain's duty to hold a service of some kind every week – indeed, it is still number one on the list of Naval Regulations, posted on every one of Her Majesty's warships. Cooke has adopted the practice of rotating the venue for 'Church' between the wardroom, the senior ratings' mess and the junior ratings' mess. This week it is the senior ratings' turn. The mess has been carefully cleared, the beer mugs put away, the hatch to the galley shut. A small band of faithful arrive in dribs and drabs – some officers, a few senior and junior ratings, fifteen in all. Finally the Captain makes another well-timed entrance, and after a short prayer the first hymn is sung, accompanied on the organ by the cassette tape recorder.

When the short service is over, the Coxswain invites the officers to stay for sherry, which he serves off a silver salver. Everyone stands around making polite conversation; one group talks shop, another proudly shows the Captain the mess's new video-recorder; he is dutifully impressed. It is a curiously formal, almost awkward scene in a social environment which is normally anything but formal and awkward.

There can be little doubt that the barrier between officers and ratings is lower on a submarine than on a surface warship. This stems partly from the living and working conditions of a submarine: there cannot be much room for formality in such a difficult environment. Indeed, it is probably true that the least formal social conditions are found on the most crowded types of submarines, the diesel-electrics, and the most formal on the massive Polaris submarines, with their luxurious L-shaped wardrooms and special 'games evenings'. But the informality may also be an indirect expression of the intense professionalism of submariners and the extent to which they rely on each other literally to stay alive.

On a surface ship, the consequences of a casual mistake by a member of the crew are unlikely to be catastrophic. A ship is basically stable; it is built to float and, barring an explosion of some kind, it will continue to provide a stable platform for its crew even if a dozen switches are incorrectly thrown, or valves opened by mistake. A submarine is not the same. By its very nature it is designed to be on a knife edge between floating and sinking. One incorrect movement of a valve or switch could spell disaster. Indeed, in the recent past one nuclear submarine came close to such an accident: an inexperienced member of the crew opened the wrong valve, and before anyone knew what was happening, the submarine was diving at an angle of 45° towards the bottom, which it avoided hitting by feet.

So standards of training are high. Apart from learning about their particular area, each trainee, both officer and rating, must be familiar with all the basic hydraulic, pumping and electrical systems of the submarine before he is awarded his 'Dolphins', the submarine's equivalent of a pilot's 'Wings'. This high degree of training is part of the reason that submariners consider themselves an élite; it must at least have the effect of weeding out most of the incompetents. A highly trained, tightly knit group of professionals, ultimately reliant on each other to stay alive, tend to abhor the artificial business of tradition – and submariners are no exception.

The Captain is still very much the revered figurehead. Everyone, including his most senior officers, calls him 'sir' or 'Captain'. Jonathan Cooke disapproves of the increasing use of Christian names amongst the officers outside the wardroom, or between officers and ratings. Like the master of any ship, he has to tread a delicate path between preserving his status and allowing some kind of a personal relationship with his crew to develop. The traditions of naval demarcation apply, in theory at least, in a submarine just as much as in a surface warship. For example, the Captain has no automatic right to enter the wardroom. The First Lieutenant is the mess president, and it is theoretically within his gift to invite the Captain to join the other officers. In a surface warship the Captain will eat his meals in solitary splendour in his cabin, and only occasionally pay a visit to the wardroom. In a submarine, this is impractical and, with the exception of breakfast, Cooke ate with his fellow officers; but he makes a point of not spending too much time sitting in the wardroom, partly because of the inhibiting effect his presence must have on his colleagues, and partly to preserve his distance from them.

'It means that one has to be self-sufficient. I'm never conscious of having experienced any particular loneliness. It's a great expression, the loneliness of command, and I think in surface ships captains must experience loneliness during long and boring periods at sea. In a submarine I don't think it's a problem for the Captain; I can withdraw to my cabin if I want to be solitary, but I can always go into the wardroom for companionship.'

Cooke glances at the photograph of his recent bride. The wedding had been delayed by *Warspite*'s extra-long patrol in the South Atlantic. 'The whole question of loneliness at sea ties in with separation from our families. Different people feel this separation in different degrees: some not at all, some very deeply. Separation generally is one of the most difficult things that servicemen, particularly in the Navy, have to deal with. We get very absorbed in what we're doing at sea, so there isn't a lot of time to brood on the loneliness and separation, but on our last record-breaking patrol people did suffer. We did get mail, but there were long delays, so people felt things were happening at home – children being born or getting sick, houses being bought – and the men felt out of touch. You take precautions if you know you're going on a long trip – hobbies, books and so on. It was remarkable how much knitting and embroidery was going on during that Falklands patrol.'

Despite his absolute involvement in the control room when the submarine is in action, the Captain does not deal very closely with the details of the submarine's daily routine. This is more the preserve of

Warspite returning to Faslane after its record-breaking South Atlantic patrol.

the First Lieutenant and the other more senior officers. If the Captain is Chairman of the Board, then David White is Managing Director. It is White who has a more obviously direct effect on the lives of the crew; he will deal with minor disciplinary offences, organise the rota for watchkeeping, give permission for films to be shown, as well as carrying out the daily inspection rounds. The 'Jimmy' tends to have to be the one who hands out bad news and the lectures on slack performances; he gets landed with the Captain's dirty work.

Submarine ratings' attitudes towards officers are mixed. By and large they tend to respect the more senior officers, but the problems occur more between the senior ratings and the junior officers. Senior ratings in the Navy are highly experienced men, whose skills and knowledge in their particular areas are very developed. They will usually stay in their job for many years, and will spend much more time at sea than their officers, who rotate between shore jobs and sea time every two to three years. This inevitably produces a situation where a senior rating will simply know more about the submarine's workings than the officer to whom he is working. Whilst most officers acknowledge this, and respect the ratings' experience, there are some young ones who do not, and indeed some senior ratings who resent having to take orders from someone younger and less knowledgeable than themselves. A significant proportion of the officers are public school, and this sometimes does not help. These problems manifest themselves largely in loud off-duty grumblings within the safety of the senior ratings' mess, but they can make difficulties for inexperienced young officers who are not too sure of their position and authority. In general, though, *Warspite* seemed a well-adjusted submarine. It comes as something of a shock to the outsider to see class divisions apparently being reinforced by such rigid adherence to rank, with stewards deferentially serving food in the wardroom; but it is the way that the services have always been and however anachronistic it may appear, it does seem to work.

The submarine service used to be all-volunteer. However, with the advent of Polaris in the early 1960s, and the increasing numbers needed to crew those and other nuclear-powered submarines, it became impossible to find sufficient volunteers. Now, although the majority of officers are volunteers to submarines, the majority of ratings are plucked from their early naval training and sent into submarines whether they like it or not. Some of them do not at first, but the Navy states that ninety per cent of ratings choose to stay with submarines after their five years' compulsory service. This is undoubtedly true, but must be partially a result of the extra pay that all submariners receive; twenty per cent on top of basic pay is an incentive that is hard to abandon.

The truth is that, extra money or not, the crew of *Warspite* were mostly a tolerant, friendly bunch of people who had clearly learnt through experience that the cramped confines of a submarine are more easily endured with a sense of humour and a degree of consideration for your colleagues. The sailors were as honest in their language and as forthright in their opinions about each other as sailors everywhere, but they did genuinely seem to have a high degree of concern for the next man. It manifested itself in small ways: the junior ratings who had the appallingly difficult job of trying to scrub the floors of the narrow, busy passageways would patiently accept that dirty shoes would keep marking their wet, clean floor, although passers-by made a significant effort to avoid doing so. In the cramped messes or the narrow passageways, in the tiny bunk spaces or the overcrowded control room, people would make an effort to get out of other people's way; and if they could not, then at least they would mutter an apology or accept the discomfort with a minimum of complaint. Even a film crew, with its disruptive trail of bits of equipment, extra bodies and constant requests for favours, was tolerated with few complaints.

It would be wrong to present every member of *Warspite*'s crew as a happy, uncomplaining saint; there were several who were quite clearly dissatisfied with their lot and were quite unwilling to conceal that dissatisfaction for the sake of their colleagues. But the answer to the often-asked question 'How do they stand it down there?' is fundamentally 'They've exploited the good old human virtues of tolerance and humour'. The relationships on *Warspite* were good; the reason was probably a combination of good luck and good management, but intangibles like those can so easily go wrong, particularly in the intense atmosphere of the hothouse society of a submarine.

Life on a submarine in comparison to a surface warship, or 'skimmer' as they are disparagingly described, has both advantages and disadvantages. The supposed extra professionalism, the pay and the informality are bonuses; the physical privations are not. Nor is the blinkered view of the world. Frigates and carriers spend what seems to submariners like most of their time on visits to glamorous faraway places. The vast majority of these ports are unavailable to nuclear-powered submarines, so the submariner's experience of foreign countries is sadly below the average sailor's. The only compensation is that, when they do get a port visit, submariners stay in comfortable hotels at the Navy's expense, rather than having to remain on board their cramped craft.

There is one other factor that binds submariners together into an élite group – their proximity to 'the enemy'. *Warspite*'s primary role in any future war would not be to sink surface ships but to detect and sink Russian submarines. It therefore follows that much of its activity during peacetime is spent preparing itself for just that. Submariners have a problem discussing this with outsiders. On the one hand, the whole question of tracking Soviet submarines is highly classified, and most of the techniques involved are secret. On the other hand, they delight in the fact that they consider themselves to be nearest to the 'front line' of any of the Services, and admit to the considerable excitement involved when tailing the opposition. It is crucially important to them to garner as much information as possible about their opponents' noise signatures, operating characteristics and tactics. So if and when *Warspite* meets a Soviet submarine, it does its utmost to follow slowly and silently behind that submarine, recording every noise it makes, identifying it through its noise signature, and noting its every move. Once positioned behind the other submarine, there may be a good chance of staying there for some time undetected. Any submerged submarine's Achilles' heel is a 90° arc behind it, in which its own noise will mask the noise of its 'tail'. Any alert submarine will occasionally slow down or turn to 'clear stern arcs', but there have been cases where the opposition has failed to do this and has given NATO submarines a golden opportunity to follow undetected. This must work both ways, of course, and it is a constant game of cat and mouse; the Royal Navy claims it comes out on top, and that no Polaris submarine, for instance, has ever been detected on patrol. This is a bold claim, and must presumably simply mean that no Soviet activity that would normally follow a detection has been noticed. Nevertheless, this deadly serious game of not-so-blind man's buff is central to the pride that many submariners have in their branch of the Royal Navy.

No Soviet submarines came close to *Warspite* during Ocean Safari. The only obvious evidence of Russian interest were two AGIs (Auxiliary-General Intelligence). These small, converted trawlers crossed our paths several times.

The exercise continues for another week, with *Warspite* making regular attacks on convoys and their escorts. Sometimes it is a long-drawn-out attack, lasting all day or all night – hours and hours of careful tracking, slowly moving into the correct position using sonar only. Sometimes we are held deep by marauding helicopters, random-dipping their sonobuoys into the water. We must simply wait until they move elsewhere – to move at any significant speed could give away our position. Sometimes the attacks themselves are carried out, not at periscope depth, but from much deeper, using our sonar as the submarine's eyes. It takes longer, and may not give quite such an accurate firing bearing and range as on periscope attacks, but the manoeuvrability of wire-guided torpedoes can compensate.

Sometimes the attacks are over more quickly, in a flurry of activity. The climax comes on the afternoon of 13 January, when *Warspite* penetrates right into the middle of an eight-ship convoy, with at least four protecting escorts also in sight. The Captain attacks the escorts and then hides amongst the convoy, picking off most of them too. He spends the afternoon with a large grin on his face.

'I haven't had an afternoon like this for years. I'm really enjoying myself.'

We finish the exercise with a tally of twelve warships, four Fleet auxiliaries and thirteen merchant ships sunk, totalling 300,000 tons. Against this, we have ourselves been detected three times, apart from the early detection by the Atlantique, and 'sunk' twice – albeit once by a frigate previously 'sunk' by us. The artificiality of the exercise becomes more and more apparent. Nevertheless, Cooke is pleased with his submarine's performance, although he acknowledges that it is a long way from the real thing.

'The exercise was good fun because we were practising our professional skills, but it would be quite different if it were for real. The adrenalin would flow even faster, and I would have quite a lot on my conscience if I'd sunk as many ships as during the carnage of the past two weeks.'

The subject of the 'real thing' and submariners' attitudes towards it are seldom spontaneously discussed in mess or wardroom. Cooke is clearly a thoughtful man, but trying to extract his inner feelings on having to fight a real war is an uphill struggle. 'We've done patrols in the South Atlantic following the Falklands war, and I've often reflected on exactly what could happen if I had to do it for real. There are all sorts of eventualities one has to consider, but as Captain of this ship I'm responsible for my own crew and their survival.'

The introduction of the Falklands as a subject naturally leads to the *Belgrano* affair. The Argentine cruiser was sunk by another, very similar submarine when *Warspite* was frantically working up to operational level after a long refit. 'It was a sobering moment for all of us when the *Belgrano* was sunk. It brought home very strongly to us that the training we were doing really was a matter of life and death. It was the first time a large ship like that had been sunk by a British submarine since the Second World War, and it made us realise just what the stakes were down in the Falklands.'

HMS *Conqueror, Warspite*'s sister submarine which sank the *General Belgrano* in the South Atlantic in May 1982.

Was there any regret amongst the ship's company about the 300 deaths? 'My ship's company felt that everyone knew there was a war going on. If you were at sea in that part of the ocean you were at risk. Being in the trade so to speak, we were aware of the weather conditions and the likely temperatures and just what it might have been like to have been in the water, just supposing you were lucky enough not to have been killed by the actual explosion. On the other hand, that action turned the whole tide of the Falklands campaign, because thereafter the Argentine Navy remained firmly in harbour.'

How would Cooke have felt if it had been he who sunk the *Belgrano*? 'A torpedo attack is a nasty business, but if I'd been that commanding officer, if *Warspite* had been in the same position, I'd have done exactly the same. I only hope I'd have done it with as much technical proficiency. I'd have done it because that was what was required to win the war, but I don't think I'd have had much pleasure in doing so.'

Members of the Commanding Officer's Qualifying Course, or Perisher, in August 1983. *From left to right:* Lt Cdr David ('Tiny') Lister, Lt José Carrera, Lt Nigel Hibbert, Lt David Charlton, Lt Cdr Gavin McClaren, Cdr Bob Stevens, Cdr Dai Evans, Lt Mike Washer, Lt Cdr Jay Plante, Lt Simon Bebbington, Lt Hank Stapel, Lt Cdr John Taubman, and the two Petty Officer Stewards, with 'Chirpy' Finch on the extreme right.

CHAPTER 2

Perisher

Early in their careers, submarine officers are split into three categories. Marine Engineers, who look after the propulsion systems, and Weapons and Electrical Engineers will reach the summit of their careers on submarines as Chief Engineers; they will never command a submarine. The third branch, Seamen Officers, do such jobs as navigating, as well as normal watchkeeping routines. In theory, every Seaman Officer can in time become captain of a submarine, and indeed for most of them that is their target. However, to reach such heights any potential submarine captain must first be recommended for the Commanding Officer's Qualifying Course – COQC or, as it is known throughout the Navy, the Perisher.

The Perisher is a five-month course which has no equal in the surface Navy. Success brings command of a submarine, or the post of First Lieutenant on a nuclear submarine, which must have two command-qualified officers. Failure certainly means never going to sea in a submarine again, except as a passenger, and probably means leaving the submarine service altogether, and possibly the Navy too. Perisher students are no chickens: the average age is over thirty, with at least ten years' submarine experience and a rank of Lieutenant or Lieutenant Commander. Failing COQC has led to nervous breakdowns and divorce, and always the stigma of 'he's a failed Perisher'. It is not difficult to understand the title – you either pass or perish. There is no second chance. About forty per cent of students fail.

There are just two courses every year, of ten or twelve students each. Of that number some will usually be from foreign navies – generally Commonwealth, but also countries with whom Britain has historical or political links, such as Holland, Brazil, Chile or Portugal, each of whom pays several thousand pounds for the privilege of sending their officers through Perisher.

It is, in fact, an extremely expensive course. After an introductory few days, the students spend three weeks in land-based submarine simulators, followed by a three-week period at sea when they are split between two submarines. During this period they work with an increasing number of frigates, until by the end they are attacking four simultaneously. Then there is another simulator period, followed by three more weeks at sea, which involves more frigates, helicopters, aircraft, and marines. It is hard to estimate costs in the Navy – to separate actual cash expenditure from running overheads – but a journalist, writing about the course, estimated the cost at £1 million per man. The Navy has not denied the figure.

On 22 August 1983, ten nervous young men and two submarine Commanders walk down a long corridor at Northwood, the Navy's headquarters in North London. At the end is a door marked 'Flag Officer Submarines'. The head of the Submarine Service is Vice-Admiral Sir John Woodward, KCB, fresh from his success in the Falklands. His secretary opens the door and announces, 'The Perisher are here to see you, sir.' Sandy Woodward rises from his desk and first greets the two commanders, Dai Evans and Bob Stevens. These are the two 'Teachers', experienced officers whose job it will be to train, judge and ultimately pass or fail the students.

The other officers file in behind them. Six from the Royal Navy, one each from Portugal, Canada, Holland and Australia. They shake hands, introduce themselves to Woodward, and sit down.

Woodward himself is a submariner. He has been through Perisher, passed, and even continued as 'Teacher'. So he understands the feelings of the students sitting in front of him. After briefly referring to his notes, he glances up at the group of nervous faces and starts to speak in quiet, deliberate tones.

'The first point I want to make is that when you become a commanding officer, your life-style changes. Suddenly you're taking life-and-death decisions for quite a lot of people at a time, and you're on your own. Perhaps most of all, you're centre stage – you have to give a command performance all the time. The question is how you get to the right standard. You have your Teacher's undivided attention for six months – and he represents an unrepeatable offer. Sometimes he won't be very communicative, he'll be tired or he will have said it all fifteen times before – but allow for that, and get everything you can out of him. The intention is that by the end, when you've qualified and you're in command of your own submarine, you may often feel lonely, you will occasionally be frightened, but you should never be surprised.

'Failure is a difficult subject, but you must face it as a possibility. We're all in the business of minimising risks – much better to learn now under guidance than later on your own with possibly fatal results. The important thing to remember is that, if you do fail, it isn't the end of your life or your career. It's traumatic at the time, but lots of people have survived it.

'Another subject I wanted to mention is stress. You will find that Teacher does stress you from time to time. It may be bloody-mindedness – that's his privilege – but it is also deliberate. We need to know your own personal limitations under pressure. Again it's another unrepeatable offer, to drive yourself and your submarine to the limits. It's an opportunity for you to find yourself, and you must use it. If you don't, you won't get through the course.'

The Perishers leave Woodward's office and walk away up the corridor, ten young men at a crossroads in their career. For the next few months their progress will be noted throughout the submarine service. In Northwood, in submarines in all parts of the world, in bars and offices in Scotland, Devonport, Portsmouth and London, wherever submariners are together, the Perisher will come up for discussion. Submarine officers are limited in number, and many of the younger ones will have worked with or at least met the six Royal Navy Perishers. Anecdotes will soon emerge, rumours about who is doing well and who is struggling. If there is a failure, the news will flash around bars and wardrooms in a matter of hours. Long faces and sympathetic phrases will treat the event more like a bereavement. It won't be dwelt upon – naval officers are not given to emotional displays – but it will be clear that they do not expect to see the unfortunate student again. If they do, they won't quite know what to say to him.

At the end of the course the lucky ones will instantly become members of an élite, albeit unofficial, club. Again, their rewards will be noted; admiration and envy will greet the news of a successful Perisher lucky enough to be 'given a drive' – command of a submarine. Sympathy will extend to those who have been given a First Lieutenant post, generally regarded as second-best.

During the course the Perisher in many ways have a privileged life. Their transport, accommodation and personal lives are looked after even more carefully than is usual in the Navy. They have none of the everyday chores of a submarine officer to worry about, such as checking the junior ratings' beer accounts. They stay in a comfortable hotel in London, rather than in naval accommodation; later, when their submarines are based at Arran, they stay in the best hotel on the island because there is so little room on the submarines.

The luxury starts on the evening of their meeting with Woodward. The entire course pay to go out for dinner in a cosy restaurant, all oak beams and brass horseshoes, in Watford High Street. Relationships over the next few months will be crucially important, both amongst students and between students and Teacher. At this stage everyone is sizing each other up, nerves on edge, hoping that their colleagues will be up to scratch, hoping that they themselves will make the grade.

At either end of the long table sits one of the two Teachers. 'Teachers' have a huge responsibility on the Perisher. Passing or failing a student is entirely their decision, with virtually no reference to anyone else. A pass sanctions a student's ability to be responsible for the lives of upwards of seventy men; a fail permanently blights his career. Dai Evans is a balding, quiet-spoken, overweight Welshman of about forty. He was previously in command of HMS *Renown*, one of the Royal Navy's four Polaris submarines. This is the second course that Evans has taught in his two-year stint as Teacher; the first course, in the spring of 1983, had a high failure rate and he is already acquiring a reputation in some quarters for being something of a martinet. At the other end of the table, Bob Stevens is in marked contrast – small, dark and mercurial, with a good line in fast wisecracks, he is less experienced than Evans, having completed the Perisher himself just four years earlier.

Both men know that the students' relationship with each other will be crucial to their success in the course. It is not a competitive course: the students will work for each other, supporting and depending on colleagues' help. It is Teachers' experience that the better the students get on with each other, the more likely they are to pass – and that one of the first signs of innate lack of ability is bickering and petty arguments. So social events like this have a point: the sooner everyone relaxes and builds up friendships, the more likely they are to be successful.

The course is split into two groups of five students, each under the command of one Teacher. Stevens' group consists of Lt Nigel Hibbert and Lt Mike Washer, plus Lt Hank Stapel, Dutch Navy, Lt Cdr Jay Plante, Canadian Navy, and Lt Cdr John Taubman from Australia. For the purpose of filming I have decided to follow just Evans' group. The senior student is 34-year-old Lt Cdr David Lister. Lister is a huge man, 6′ 4″ and weighing at least fifteen stone. In truly original Naval slang he is therefore known as 'Tiny'. With his black beard and forceful voice, Tiny's presence is impossible to ignore in any situation; it is difficult to believe he can physically fit into a submarine control room. He joined the Navy fifteen years ago and made the unusual switch from Marine Engineer to Seaman Officer in mid-career, having failed an important engineering examination. He started the previous Perisher course, but had to drop out with a

Cdr Dai Evans.

'Tiny' Lister before he was promoted to Lt Cdr.

Lt Simon Bebbington in the submarine control room.

Lt David Charlton.

mysterious stomach complaint. Later that evening he looked back on the earlier engineering failure and acknowledged that it had probably prepared him for the possibility of not passing Perisher.

Next to Lister sits Lt Simon Bebbington, 32, and with eleven years of submarine experience behind him. Like most of his colleagues, Bebbington looks less impressive in civilian clothes than he did in the afternoon in his naval uniform, and it is hard to imagine him as a submarine captain. He speaks quickly, nervously and with a very slight Devon twang, and betrays his nervousness by laughing a little too easily and too often.

Next comes Lt Cdr Gavin McClaren, also 32, but with fourteen years of naval experience. He is small, fair-haired and already balding, with deep-set eyes and a quiet manner. Like Bebbington, it is hard to imagine him in command. Later in the evening he speculated on the magic ingredients needed to be a successful leader of men, citing the example of a particular commanding officer with whom he had served. He confessed that he just didn't know whether he had those qualities or not.

The only foreign member of this half of the course is Lt José Carrera from the Portuguese Navy. He is unable to be at this dinner, so the only other student in Evans' group is Lt David Charlton, 30, the youngest in the group. Tall, fair-haired and well built, Charlton on the face of it looks most like a potential submarine captain. But he seems shy and unself-confident, speaking hesitantly and nervously. Both he and McClaren are talking mostly to Dai Evans, who sits at their end of the table. Keen to make a good impression, yet conscious that this is an informal, social occasion, the students' conversation to their Teacher is a mixture of shop-talk and anecdote. Evans is impatient to get to know his students; he found the last course difficult but has hopes that this group may be more enjoyable. At this stage, neither Teacher has any idea of what will happen. There is no written examination to pass, no set of marks against which the students can be judged. The only standard is that set by the two Teachers; it is their judgement that controls the future of the men around the table. It could be that all will pass – or none. Any one of the ten green bottles could fall off the wall at any time in the next few months.

After a series of mainly informational visits to various naval establishments, and a look round Barr and Stroud, makers of the Navy's periscopes, the Perisher starts work properly on the morning of 29 August with Bob Stevens' group in Portsmouth and Dai Evans' group at the Clyde Submarine Base in Faslane.

The purpose of the Perisher course is threefold. First and foremost, Teacher has to satisfy himself that his students are capable of safeguarding their submarine and the lives of its crew in any conceivable situation, whether at peace or in war, but in particular when carrying out an attack on a surface ship. Secondly, he must be satisfied that they can carry out the operational requirements of the submarine, whatever kind of operations those may be, from torpedo attacks to covert, inshore night operations. Thirdly, he must satisfy himself that the student is capable of leading, and keeping the confidence of, his crew.

The first two requirements can be taught; the student's ability to perform them satisfactorily depends principally on his mental powers, and how much effort he is prepared to devote to acquiring the expertise. The third can only be taught to a limited extent. The question of whether an officer either has command presence or not is one that the Perisher is designed to answer. The immediate requirement, though, is that the students should be taught to keep their submarine safe, and at the same time operational. To this end, the first half of the Perisher course is based on teaching them how to carry out torpedo attacks on enemy ships.

They start to learn this by working in a submarine control-room simulator. Known as the Attack Trainer, this has all the features and equipment of a real control room, but is larger and therefore easier to move around in. It has a computerised system, operated by a Wren, which simulates the submarine's propulsion, steering and diving controls. The same computer controls the movements of a model frigate in front of a TV camera, which provides a video image which the student can see through the periscope. The computer also feeds sonar information into the simulated sound room, where ratings operate sonar equipment which exactly matches the equipment on a submarine. There is even a loudspeaker system which reproduces the noise of ships passing close overhead. A screen in front of the Wren displays the simulator submarine's position in relation to the other ships.

For the first few days the computer is programmed to run a series of single-ship attacks. What this means in effect is that a frigate, travelling at anything up to thirty knots, will approach the submarine. It may charge straight for the submarine, or it may turn away, or do one of a dozen different manoeuvres. What the student captain must do is manoeuvre his submarine, at periscope depth, into a position where he can fire a torpedo, 'hit' the warship and himself remain safe. It is a similar process to what Jonathan Cooke was doing on *Warspite* during Ocean Safari – but with one important difference. The student is in a simulated diesel-electric submarine, whose underwater speed is limited to a fraction of *Warspite*'s maximum. The difference between the speed of the submarine and its target means the student captain must try and anticipate what the frigate is going to do, and place himself in the correct position to fire, because he will only get one opportunity. With a combined closing speed of up to forty mph, and a maximum visibility of about eight miles, the student has about fifteen

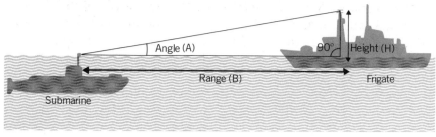

Establishing the course and speed of the target. (Not to scale.)

minutes to carry out each attack. Once he has identified that a hostile ship is approaching him, he must carry out a series of calculations and operations that will both keep his submarine safe and allow him to attack.

Firstly, he must calculate the course and speed of the ship. He does this by taking both bearings and ranges; from this information his plotters can soon tell him which direction the frigate is heading and how fast. Bearings are simply the angle from the submarine at which the submarine is approaching, and are read off a 360° scale when the periscope is pointed precisely at the frigate. Taking a range is more complex. There is a split-image device within the periscope which allows the student to raise a second image of the target above the true image. When the waterline of the raised image is placed at the top of the real ship's masts, the student calls out for his periscope assistant to read off the resulting angle in fractions of a degree, or minutes of arc. He can then effectively draw an imaginary triangle whose base is a line between his periscope and the waterline of the target and whose apex is the top of the target's mast. He knows the angle at the submarine's end of the triangle, he knows that the angle at the other end of the base-line is a right angle, and he can therefore calculate the third angle in the triangle. He will by now have identified the ship attacking him, and will consequently know from memory how high the masts are from the waterline. So with all three angles and the length of one side, he can calculate the length of the triangle's base-line, which is of course the range.

He does this by using one of two mathematical formulae – either $h \div a \times 1150$ or $hv \div a \times 1000$, both of which give him the range in yards. Here h is the height of the mast, a is the angle at the periscope end of the triangle, and v is a constant 1.15 which converts true height into virtual height and – in theory at least – slightly simplifies the equation by allowing the constant 1150 to become the constant 1000. So if, for example, the height of the mast is known to be sixty feet, and the angle happens to be sixteen minutes, the student must make the calculation $60 \div 16 \times 1150$, or $60 \div 16 \times 1.15 \times 1000$, both of which result in a range of 4300 yards. In addition, taking precise timings as the ranges are taken, the speed of the target can be calculated as the range diminishes. These mental equations must, of course, be done at lightning speed, and in turn lead on to other complex calculations which also involve instantaneous mental arithmetic.

Having established the course and speed of the target, the next priority for the student is to ensure that it is at a safe distance from him. The primary threat to his submarine's safety stems from the assumption the student must make that at any moment the target may identify him, and turn directly towards him with the intention of ramming. If the target does this, the student must allow sufficient time to dive his submarine to a safe depth. When working against the frigates, this depth is ninety feet from the submarine's keel to the surface which, allowing for the height of the submarine and the draught of the frigate, will leave a ten- to fifteen-foot gap between the two craft as the frigate thunders overhead.

The diesel-electric submarines in which the student is working have a large ballast tank near the bows, called 'Q' tank, which is normally kept empty. It can rapidly be flooded with five tons of water which, when combined with maximum angle on the foreplanes, will dive the submarine to ninety feet in sixty seconds. Knowing this timing, the student can proceed to calculate the proximity of the target to what's called the 'go-deep circle'. This is a notional lozenge-shaped area of water around the submarine which, if penetrated by the target, will force him to duck down to ninety feet. The extent of the go-deep circle depends on the target's speed combined with the submarine's own speed and the direction from which the target is approaching.

If, for example, the target is approaching at thirty knots head on to the submarine, which in turn is travelling at six knots, the closing speed is thirty-six knots. The student must first convert this closing speed into yards per minute. A thirty-six-knot combined closing speed is in fact 1200 yards per minute, so the student knows that the extent of his go-deep circle – in other words, the minimum distance he can allow the target to approach before he must give the order to flood 'Q' tank and allow sixty seconds to get to a safe depth – is 1200 yards. This go-deep circle varies in size depending on the direction from which the target is approaching. If the target is coming from dead astern, the closing speed will not be thirty knots plus six knots, but thirty knots minus six knots, or twenty-four knots, and it will therefore take the target sixty seconds to cover a shorter distance – in this case approximately 900 yards. If the target is approaching from the side, the go-deep circle will be about 1000 yards at these speeds.

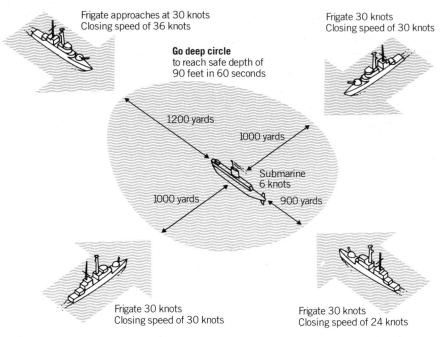

Frigate approaches at 30 knots
Closing speed of 36 knots

Frigate 30 knots
Closing speed of 30 knots

Go deep circle
to reach safe depth of
90 feet in 60 seconds

1200 yards

1000 yards

Submarine
6 knots

1000 yards

900 yards

Frigate 30 knots
Closing speed of 30 knots

Frigate 30 knots
Closing speed of 24 knots

During an attack the student must therefore take frequent ranges on the target, which he must then relate to the range of the go-deep circle – which of course may also be constantly changing if the target changes speed or approaches from a different direction. The difference between these two ranges must then be converted into time in order to give the student his 'look interval'.

The look interval is the amount of time he can safely allow between each raising of the periscope to check the progress of the target. Obviously he cannot keep the periscope up constantly, because of the increased likelihood of detection. Let us assume that the speed of the frigate is thirty knots, and it is coming straight towards the submarine which is travelling at six knots. The student takes a range angle – say, sixteen minutes of a degree. Using the formula $hv \div a \times 1000$ he calculates the range is 4300 yards. The go-deep circle at this closing speed and bearing is 1200 yards. Using two pieces of Perisher mental arithmetic shorthand, the student now calculates the look interval. He divides the go-deep circle range into the target range (4300 ÷ 1200 = 3, remainder 700). He calculates the 'range rate' of the ship by dividing the combined closing speed into 180 (180 ÷ 36 = 5). He then multiplies this number by the remainder from the range division calculation (5 × 700 = 3500) and divides it by 100 (3500 ÷ 100 = 35), which gives him the number of seconds to add on to the full three minutes which the 4300 ÷ 1200 calculation produced. All he now has to do is subtract one minute and, lo and behold, he has reached the look interval – in this case 2′ 25″, or 145 precious seconds during which he can, in theory, forget that particular ship, concentrate on other problems in the attack, and be absolutely certain that it will not violate his go-deep circle. As the course progresses, and more frigates are deployed to attack the submarine simultaneously, the student must calculate the ranges, bearings and look intervals of up to four ships, all of which have to be constantly updated every few seconds. The student uses a multitude of stopwatches to remind him when his look intervals are due: one around his neck, one hanging from the ceiling, one on each wrist.

At the same time he must cope with many other factors, two of which are crucial. He must remember every few minutes to take an 'all-round look', a quick 360° sweep of the periscope to make sure that no other ships have emerged from the distance to threaten him whilst he has been concentrating on his target. He must also calculate exactly when to fire his torpedo salvo, and what deflection angle to allow for the relative angle of his submarine and the target.

Since the ultimate purpose of this part of the course is to ensure that the Perisher student is capable of keeping his submarine and its seventy crew safe under the most testing circumstances, the most important decision for each student during his attack is whether or when to go deep. As the target approaches the go-deep circle, the student must keep his nerve. To go deep too early may be very safe but renders the submarine useless. To delay too long is potentially dangerous and goes down in Teacher's notebook as a black mark. The target's courses are designed to make this decision as hard as possible for the student. Sometimes the frigate will steam straight at the submarine, without deviating from its course – in which case it's fairly obvious what the student has to do, as long as his ranges are correct. But as often as not the target will be programmed to 'skirt' or 'squeeze' the submarine. The skirt is a wicked manoeuvre wherein the frigate will start by charging straight towards the submarine, but just as it is about to force the student to go deep it alters course and moves around the submarine, hugging the very edge of the go-deep circle. The student must watch the frigate extremely closely for any suggestion that it is changing course towards him, taking ranges every few seconds. The squeeze is a manoeuvre for two frigates, and again involves them charging straight at the submarine. At the last moment they both alter course – one to port and one to starboard – so that they just touch the go-deep circle. The student must again keep his nerve for as long as possible as they approach.

So the pattern that emerges from the fifteen-minute attacks is a quiet start, with the initial sighting of the target prompting the

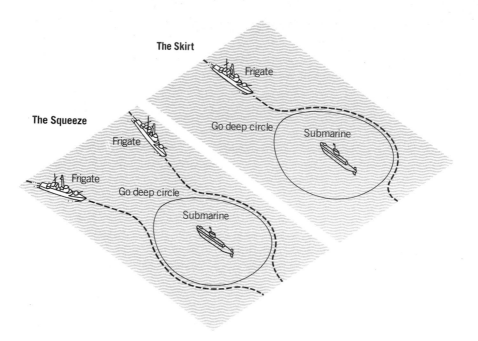

The Skirt

Frigate

The Squeeze

Frigate

Frigate

Go deep circle

Submarine

Go deep circle

Submarine

Perisher to announce its presence and his intention of attacking. A steady stream of bearings and ranges follow, which enable the plotters to calculate course and speed. If the student has misread the frigate's course, and not manoeuvred his own submarine into the correct position, the attack may fizzle out as the frigate steams past thousands of yards away, leaving the slow-moving diesel-electric submarine watching helplessly. But if the submarine is correctly placed, the frigate will be coming closer and closer.

Now the attack builds to its climax. The student must give his torpedo-firing team as much information about the target's course and speed as possible, and he must prepare for the possibility of having to go deep. Flooding 'Q' tank is a routine which needs certain controls to be set up already, and the student must warn his control room if he intends to do this manoeuvre. So, long before his go-deep circle is penetrated, the Perisher must call out 'Stand-by Q, stand-by Q routine' – and indeed if he hasn't done this within about thirty seconds of potentially being forced deep, Teacher will call it out for him.

When he is at a satisfactory distance and angle from the target, the captain can fire his torpedoes – although it was to happen more than once during the following weeks that the student became so involved in providing the data for the torpedo firing, as well as concentrating on whether or not he should go deep, that he entirely forgot to fire his salvo – the whole point of the attack. The other peak of the attack is the moment of decision about going deep. If he decides to do it, the Perisher will call out, 'Full ahead together, Flood Q, wheel amidships, keep ninety feet,' and the submarine (or simulator display) will safely duck under the advancing escort.

It all adds up to a maelstrom of activity, which leaves the students literally dripping with sweat and mentally exhausted. This punishing exercise naturally raises questions of artificiality. Firstly, the likelihood of up to four frigates attacking a submarine simultaneously disappeared at the end of the last war; modern submarine warfare would probably never lead to such a situation. Secondly, forcing the student to carry out endless complex mental calculations seems perverse almost to the point of cruelty when a simple electronic calculator would solve the problem. A submarine is, after all, packed with sophisticated electronic equipment.

The Navy justifies this pressure by claiming that it is vital that the students should demonstrate that they have the mental capacity to do these calculations whilst retaining the ability to think clearly about the tactics involved in dealing with a multi-ship attack. Dai Evans explains:

'Some aspects of the course are slightly artificial, but in order to be able to test someone and prove them fully capable of taking the responsibility of command just in safety terms, it's important that you take them to the limits. We create these kinds of situations so that the student is aware of his limitations and is then unlikely to exceed them in his first period of command. Obviously once you are actually in command, you benefit from the experience of being there and you can refine the techniques that you use, and the way in which you handle the submarine, and you gradually achieve better and better results. But the aim is that at the end of the Perisher course, the embryo commanding officer should be able to take his submarine to war.'

By the end of their first three days in the simulator, the embryo commanding officers are feeling somewhat chastened. They all take it in turns to be duty captain, and to command the simulator; the rest carry out other functions in the control room, such as plotting course and speed, or co-ordinating the torpedo-fire control system. The student who has just completed an attack takes a rest and observes his successor's efforts. They are all still feeling their way, conscious that they are right at the beginning of a long haul, and that the difficulties they are currently experiencing will be nothing as compared to the complexities of multi-ship attacks at sea rather than single-ship attacks in a simulator. What is already emerging is the need to be self-critical as well as to accept criticism from Teacher. Evans sits, hawk-eyed, at the control desk, watching every move the student captain makes, occasionally firing out a phrase of criticism, encouragement or advice, and making notes about each attack as it progresses. Although he knows in advance what the computer has programmed the target to do – indeed he can actually see it displayed on a screen in front of him – Evans still works out many of the ranges and look intervals in his head, and it is noticeable how much quicker he is than the students. If a student is a few hundred yards out on his range, or a few seconds inaccurate on his look interval, Evans will instantly fire in a correction.

After each attack, Evans goes through the problems with all the students in a huddle, whilst the ratings and Wrens who control the equipment sit quietly and have a cigarette. At this stage Evans is striving to teach the students the basic techniques of submarine handling, drawing on his own wide experience. It is still too early to make a clear judgement about individuals' progress – although one student is already causing him some concern.

José, the Portuguese, is finding it difficult to cope with the extra problem of carrying out the mental calculations in a foreign language, as well as understanding the reports from the plot-table about the target's movements. His attacks are not going well, and he is even proving something of a liability when carrying out the supportive duties to other student captains. He occasionally raises his eyes to the ceiling in frustration, where he catches sight of a sign that a previous Chilean student wrote: 'Querer es poder' – 'To want to is to be able to'. José knows that that student passed the Perisher, and he is trying hard to do the same.

Every evening, after their day's attacking, the students are debriefed by Evans and then sit quietly for a while discussing their progress.

Simon: It feels great when you've done an attack which you think has gone well. There may be lots of faults in it, but as long as you can identify them, that's OK – the self-criticism part is important.

Tiny: I think the trouble with doing a bad attack is the fact that everybody has 20/20 hindsight, so you look at the plots and the log-sheets afterwards and you think, my God – did I really do that? It looks so pedestrian and stupid.

David: You actually do your best attacks when you're not duty captain, but when you're just observing someone else. You've got the time to get all the maths right and you know exactly what you should be doing. One of the difficult things is, if you do a bad attack, you've got to be able to put it behind you and not let it depress you. You must think OK, learn from that one, don't get down about it, the next one will be a good one. You've got to keep that positive feeling in your mind otherwise after two or three bad attacks you could really plummet downhill.

The students are all trying hard to minimise the importance of the course they are on. It is a natural defence mechanism, when faced with such a major hurdle, to convince yourself that it would not really matter if you failed. But the genuine concern, anxiety and commitment to the course easily break through.

Simon: For seven or eight years in submarines, you've been going up the ladder in different jobs, with the ultimate goal that if you're good enough you'll get selected for Perisher.

Gavin: It overrides everything else – one's domestic life, for instance. Both David and I live locally, and our wives will tell you that you're not a very nice person to know for the five months of the course because you're putting that first. One thing that does strike me is that if you pass this course, in your early thirties, someone is actually going to give you this fantastically expensive, complex and potentially powerful weapon to command. You know – there you are, it's yours, off you go, we think you're good enough to take this submarine. It's just unbelievable that somebody will actually give me one of those things to command.

Simon: That's right – it's all yours, and there's going to be nobody standing behind you saying you didn't do that very well.

A week later, the first casualty hit the course. José, despite valiant efforts, was slowly becoming bogged down in his inability to communicate. He was, as Evans put it, to all intents and purposes deaf in the control room. Originally a cheerful and smiling man, he had slowly become more and more miserable as the course progressed. His attacks were muddled and he was becoming a liability to the other students. Evans finally decided that he would have to go, and the sooner the better – not least because an early retirement from the course for obvious language reasons would carry less ignominy than a later failure for more fundamental reasons. When Teacher told him the bad news, he reported that José felt a sense of relief – and smiled for the first time since the attacks began.

Then there were nine . . .

Both Teacher and students were sorry to see José leave the course, but he had not stayed long enough to make it a real wrench. Later on, when a close relationship has developed amongst the students, a failure is more traumatic. This relationship is already developing, both on and off duty. It is noticeable in the simulator how supportive the Perishers are to the duty captain. Apart from doing their best to provide him with the basic information he needs, they will try and slip in a few extras. If the Perisher on the LOP (Local Operations Plot) spots the beginning of a possible zigzag by the target on his chart, he'll tell the duty captain immediately: 'Possible zig to port.' The Attack Co-ordinator will have brief, shorthand conversations with the duty captain at the most critical time of the attack, during which probably rather more concealed advice is given than would normally flow from First Lieutenant to Captain. Teacher knows this is happening, and sees nothing wrong in it. He's glad that such a good relationship is developing – and at the same time it is useful to him to see exactly who needs the most help.

Away from the simulator, the four officers often stick together in the informal back bar at the Faslane wardroom, sometimes with Evans, sometimes not. There have been Perisher courses in the past where the relationship between the students became one of rivalry and bitterness, with every man for himself. These tend to be the less successful courses. However corny it may sound, Perisher is a team effort – at the very least it is a waste of precious energy and conversation to worry about the others' success.

The Perishers' relationship with their Teacher is developing too. Dai Evans is turning out to be a most interesting and unusual man. He rose from the ranks to become an officer, subsequently passed his own Perisher with honours, and finished up commanding a Polaris submarine. His thin-lipped, rather impassive face seems to reflect his brusque, no-nonsense manner with ratings and Perisher alike. During each attack Evans watches, concentrating, his jaw rhythmically moving as he works a tiny muscle in his cheek. He is tough, demanding and relentless in his pursuit of perfection. But it would be a mistake to take the superficial reading of his character as the only one. Away from the simulator he becomes a different person, laughing, joking and liking nothing more than to have a beer with his students. He manages to be close to them, relaxed and informal – yet still maintains his role as Teacher, with an indefinable air of reserve or formality at the right moment.

With such a small group to control, there must always be the danger of favouritism or flattery distorting judgement, but Evans is fully aware of each student's insistence on buying the drinks, and succeeds in deflecting the problem by making a joke out of it. He is totally committed to the submarine service and to his role as Teacher. Teaching and hopefully passing his students is all-important to him and, despite his hard exterior, he dreads the possibility of having to fail someone. A rating who works close to him once observed that, underneath, Evans was really 'just a big softie'. He certainly disliked having to fail so many on the previous course, but he is only beginning to have an idea of whether that will be necessary this time.

After three weeks in the simulator, at the end of which the Perisher have been coping with four-ship attacks, there is one student who is just beginning to cause Evans some concern. Gavin McClaren carries out very confident attacks, and in many ways is the most competent of the four, although he does occasionally have a disaster. Simon Bebbington and David Charlton are both progressing well, although David's hesitant nature sometimes gives the impression of uncertainty. The fourth student, the huge Tiny Lister, is the only one beginning to struggle. Tiny has difficulty creating a mental picture of the relationship between submarine and target, and therefore his manoeuvres are too often clumsy and late. The endless calculations throw him. His massive, bearded face screws up with the concentration needed to avoid getting all the different problems muddled. But Evans is not yet seriously concerned about Tiny – there is still plenty of time for him to improve.

After three weeks in the simulator, the entire Perisher course moves to Arran. The action in the next three weeks will be confined to the twenty-mile-wide strip of Clyde between Arran and the Scottish mainland. This has always been a busy training area for submarines. The water is deep, but there are plenty of hazards to test the embryo captain, such as the Brodick-Ardrossan car ferry and endless small fishing boats.

Everyone assembles at Kilcreggan Pier, a few miles from Faslane, on the afternoon of 19 September. It is a foul day, with a strong wind blowing and heavy showers of cold rain. Rocking uneasily in the increasing swell is the fast launch *Osprey*, her two Rolls-Royce engines throbbing quietly as she waits at the end of the jetty. The southern half of the Perisher have flown up to join Dai Evans' group, and the conversation is full of excited accounts of the past three weeks, comparing experiences in quick, jargon-packed sentences.

We head for Arran at twenty knots and immediately start pitching violently in the swell. Sheets of spray fly out to the side as the bows crash down on every wave; the journey becomes an adventure. It is appropriate that it should, because the next day is when the real adventure of Perisher begins. Simulators, with their video images through the periscope, their comfortable size and their unreality, are behind the course now. As we approach Arran, HMS *Oracle*, the diesel-electric submarine on which Simon, Tiny, Gavin and David will work for the next three weeks, emerges from the mist. Low, sleek and black, *Oracle* too is pitching heavily as she ploughs towards Arran. The spray from her bows must be soaking the watchkeepers on the bridge. The students watch her intently. They've seen submarines dozens of times before, they've all served on them for years – but this is different. Tomorrow *Oracle* will be theirs to command.

As we slow down in Brodick Bay, the lean, grey shape of the Leander-class anti-submarine frigate HMS *Euryalus* slips in from the south, completing the scenario. The next day will be all reality: a real target, a real submarine, and all the unpredictability of fishing boats, weather and a hundred different potential problems.

Low clouds cover the top of the green hills that surround the bay. The rain lashes down in torrents. *Osprey* noses alongside the jetty,

HMS *Oracle*, which Perisher 2/83 will remember for many years.

and the Perishers scramble up on to not very dry land. A quick walk brings them to the welcome warmth of the Douglas Hotel, where they will stay for the next three weeks.

The Douglas Hotel has housed the Perisher for many years, and the owner, Jim Halluck, is delighted with the business it brings. Ten young men under a degree of pressure like to relax in the evenings, along with the two Teachers and guests from the submarines and frigates, as well as visiting naval dignitaries from the mainland. So the specially named 'Perisher Bar' in the basement is a tribute to the business the course has brought him. Around the walls are painted the names of all the Navy's diesel-electric submarines; on one is a huge mural of a submarine in action, and there is a written testimony to the Perisher which reads:

The waters surrounding this island of Arran are frequently visited by the crews and submarines of the navies of the free world, and in particular those who aspire to become commanding officers of these submarines.

We are honoured to play host to those gentlemen, affectionately known as 'The Perishers' and wish them every success in their ventures.

The working schedule for the Perisher and their Teachers is a punishing one. Next morning and every morning thereafter, they rise at about 5 am and leave the hotel by 5.45. A fleet tender – much like a small tug – is waiting at the jetty to take them out to the two submarines anchored in the bay. Dawn is barely breaking as they loom out of the darkness, black silhouettes merging with the inky water. Quiet and pensive now, the excited chatter of the previous day over, Dai Evans and his four students climb on to the narrow, slippery casing and walk along to the main access hatch. They clamber down the ladder and emerge in the warm, impossibly cramped interior of HMS *Oracle*.

To the newcomer, the inside of a diesel-electric submarine is everything he both expected and feared. The design dates from the 1950s, and they are not much bigger than the last of Germany's wartime U-boats. The interior makes *Warspite* look absurdly wasteful of space. Like *Warspite*, the basic layout is torpedoes in the fore-ends, control room in the middle and engine room at the stern. But unlike *Warspite* there is only one level – and one long continuous passageway which snakes tortuously from bow to stern. There are seventy men on board, and although they all have their own bunk, there is no single area which matches the bunk space of *Warspite* – nowhere dedicated to sleeping. Bunks are crammed in to every nook and cranny – along passageways, doubling as seats around dining tables, tucked into impossible corners in the engine room. The wardroom is about half the size of *Warspite*'s, and although it has to accommodate fewer officers – seven as opposed to thirteen – it does have to provide bunk and storage space for four of them. The table seats a maximum of six, so mealtimes with the additional Perisher officers are a complex routine. Two of the other officers sleep in bunks elsewhere in the submarine – one in the passageway outside the wardroom. The Captain, as on all submarines, has the luxury of his own cabin. It is placed just aft of the control room and, although tiny, is a precious sanctuary of privacy and personal lebensraum.

Clambering through circular, watertight hatches, smelling diesel fuel in the atmosphere, coping with the awkward confines of the tiny lavatories, whose low ceiling turns urinating into a contortionist's act, the visitor acknowledges this as the 'real' world of submarines, and wonders how men stand it for weeks on end.

HMS *Oracle* is driven by a huge battery – the equivalent of 15,000 ordinary car batteries – which takes up much of the space under the floor. This battery will provide electricity for a limited period only. Depending on the speed of the submarine, it could be anything from a few hours to several days. The submarine has two powerful diesel engines which can recharge the battery within hours. But of course to run them needs fresh air, and therein lies the inherent weakness of the diesel-electric submarine. It must either surface to run its engines, which hugely increases its vulnerability, or it can use a technique invented by the Germans in the Second World War – snorting. Snorting involves raising a two-foot-diameter pipe above the surface while the submarine is at periscope depth; through this pipe fresh air can be sucked to feed the diesels. But even a small protuberance above the surface can be detected by radar – and of course the diesels themselves are very noisy – so these submarines are inherently more vulnerable than the nuclear-powered vessels. However, when running submerged on its battery, the diesel-electric is the most difficult type of all submarines to detect. It can, if required, go absolutely silent by switching off all non-vital equipment and stopping its screw, leaving the submarine suspended in the water. A nuclear submarine cannot switch off its reactor-cooling pumps and, despite the engineers' best efforts, these will always make a noise.

Absolute silence and avoiding detection is the last thing on the Perishers' minds this morning. HMS *Euryalus* knows exactly where they are, because Teacher has just flashed a message pinpointing the submarine's position and announcing that he is ready for the first attack run.

Tiny Lister is the senior student on this half of the course, so the doubtful privilege of taking command of the submarine through diving and the first attack has fallen to him. He stands, tense and nervous, by the attack periscope, waiting for the frigate to emerge from the grey gloom and mist of the Clyde. Behind him, Dai Evans takes up his position by the search periscope. In a tiny bunk space beyond the wardroom, known as the 'Goatshed', the other three students sit, nerves jangling. The first attack, they all agree, is by far the worst. Simon Bebbington is feeling physically ill with nervous anticipation – his face is grey and sweating, his hands and fingers move constantly in a flurry of twitches. 'I shall be so glad when this first one's over,' he admits. 'It's a feeling of unmitigated terror. I know I can do the mechanics of it – but this is a real-life submarine. We've all handled a periscope before, so none of that's new, it's just that suddenly you're there, you're the one who's doing it all as opposed to sitting back and watching.'

In the control room, Tiny has seen the frigate through his periscope, but is hesitating to start the attack run. Teacher is getting impatient. 'Why haven't we started the attack, Captain?' he asks irritably. Tiny announces that he intends to attack, gives the details of what he hopes to do in terms of the torpedo salvo, and the run is on.

Back in the goatshed Gavin is chain-smoking, greedily sucking in lungfuls of smoke. 'What's going through my mind? Trying to remember all the things we've been taught, hoping I don't make a complete fool of myself. Just keeping my fingers crossed, and remembering to keep my elbows tucked well into my sides so the ship's company can't see how much my arms are shaking. You have to put on an act. However nervous and dreadful you feel, you can't let it show – you've got to appear calm and confident when in fact you're in a mental turmoil.'

Suddenly the huge bulk of Tiny Lister stumbles in and clambers onto the bench seat. The others listen enviously.

'Thank God that's over. It was a bit confusing really. The weather's quite good so I could see him clearly, but I was expecting more to happen instead of him trundling past. I was waiting, thinking – Is he going to alter course? Is he going to put me deep? I kept looking, but nothing happened. It wasn't a great attack, but it's given me a feel for what the periscope is like.'

Lister thankfully drinks a cup of coffee and settles down to check through his log-sheet, which contains the details of how often he raised the periscope, and what information he gained from it each time. Bulky sheets of tracing paper from the chart-table also tell him the course of the submarine and target as they closed together.

Now it's Gavin's turn. As he walks into the control room he appears quite confident – it is not clear how tightly his elbows are tucked into his sides. Fifteen minutes later he is back in the goatshed with a grin all over his face.

'Right – I feel much better for that. It's really very nice to do one and discover how much you can see through the periscope. It's not too difficult really, it just gets rid of the nervous butterflies in the stomach. The most difficult thing about it was that the water takes time to drain off the top window of the periscope. So when you first put the periscope up you have a very fuzzy picture, and you have to force yourself to wait until it drains before you take a range. I enjoyed it, that's the best thing I can say, whereas ten minutes ago I was dreading it. Where are my cigarettes?'

David Charlton and Simon Bebbington also complete their first attacks without mishap, and the students gradually settle into their routine. As in the simulator, they take it in turns to be duty captain, followed by one attack run spent analysing their log-sheets and plots, then a spell either as attack co-ordinator, squashed into the torpedo-firing end of the control room, or on the CEP (Contact Evaluation Plot) which registers the movements of the target and other craft in the area.

The attacks continue without interruption until darkness falls. The lone frigate on the surface careers up and down the Clyde, working both with HMS *Oracle* and with the other half of the course, a few miles to the south, in HMS *Otter*. The skill of the frigate's commanding officer is essential to the training value of the attack run. Dai Evans and Bob Stevens have arranged with him that every run should have a slightly different pattern, so that the students never know what to expect. The precision with which the frigate carries out these runs has to be very fine. A last-minute turn towards the submarine must be executed at exactly the right range in order to test the students' nerve and technique; if the frigate is to carry out a skirting manoeuvre, it must hug the edge of the go-deep circle very closely. The submarine keeps its wireless mast raised above the surface at all times, to give a constant marker and ranging point for the frigate, but in the choppy grey Firth of Clyde it can still be very hard to pick out this pinpoint of steel.

Although the students take it in turns, the two Teachers must effectively do every single attack – and there are as many as twenty runs in a single day. Although Evans knows what the frigate is going to do, he is nevertheless responsible for the safety of the submarine, and so he must at all times be absolutely clear as to where the frigate is. And, since he must also project himself into the mind of the student Captain, Teacher doesn't simply leave his search periscope up all the time but matches the student's procedure by raising the periscope and taking ranges and bearings, exactly as if he were doing the attack. So inside the control room, as each attack develops, a kind of rhythmic, almost balletic, dance for two periscopes unfolds.

The two periscope hoist operators stand, side by side, at the rear of the control room, their hands constantly poised on the polished brass levers that control the hydraulic systems that raise and lower the two heavy periscopes in seconds. The student calls out 'Raise attack' or 'Lower attack'; Teacher simply gestures with a flick of his hand when he wants the search periscope raised, and snaps the handles up when he's finished with it. The student calls out when his split image is correctly placed, his assistant calls back the minutes, the student calculates the range, calls that out, and then the look interval. Meanwhile Evans looks at the minutes for himself and calculates the range and look interval, but does not call them out. If the student has made an error, Teacher will snap out 'Bad range', and the student must try again.

When the frigate is close, Teacher must be prepared to take over command of the submarine if the student gets in a muddle and delays going deep for too long. This is the tensest time of all; the student knows that he must not go deep too soon, since this would be overcautious – but at all costs he wants to avoid overstepping the limit. For Teacher to have to take the decision to 'Flood Q' is a significant black mark against the safety capabilities of the student. So his ranges must be absolutely accurate – and he must work them out very fast. When the frigate is just a few hundred yards outside the go-deep circle, the look intervals are down to a matter of seconds, so the two periscopes are constantly raised and lowered, virtually simultaneously, and the mental tension of student and Teacher is palpable.

Despite his much greater experience, this constant pressure puts a great strain on Teacher. Evans' concentration never flickers for an instant. The tension again sets that muscle in his jaw working, and he occasionally snaps at the periscope hoist operator if he's slow, or at the officer in charge of depth-keeping if he goes too deep and submerges the periscope head – or indeed at anyone who gets in the way as he swings the periscope around. At the end of each attack there may be time for a quick cigarette before the frigate turns and starts its next run. After every second attack there is a forty-minute break whilst the frigate runs back and forth past the other submarine, and Teacher will try to squeeze in a debrief with the students about their last run – or maybe snatch a cup of coffee.

At the end of the first day of three weeks of this punishing routine, the submarine slips quietly back into Brodick Bay. The Perisher and their Teacher gather up their papers, walk wearily along the casing, and jump across into the waiting tender, as the last glimmer of evening light fades from the sky. It's nearly thirteen hours since they boarded the submarine. The tender collects the rest of the students from HMS *Otter* and heads for the jetty. On the bridge, the two Teachers quietly compare notes and agree that, considering it was the first day, it has been quite satisfactory – no major mishaps, no breakdowns.

Evans is already beginning to put the students in a pecking order. The trends that he started to pick out in the simulator have been confirmed on this first day at sea.

'Two of them have done good attacks; one of them is not doing all that well; and the fourth is actually beginning to struggle. But as time goes on they should get more comfortable, and I'm not going to give up on anybody. The aim is to qualify as many commanding officers as we have students on this course.'

The students walk on up to the Douglas Hotel, eager for a bath and dinner. The relief of surviving their first day at sea produces jokes, laughs, shouts of pleasure, which hide any lingering worries about their performance.

Dai Evans: 'What I'm looking for in a potential commanding officer is somebody with professional competence and professional honesty. What I'm also looking for is someone who has the ability to motivate

The Perisher course has been going for over sixty years. These successful Perishers of 1936 are standing behind the squashed remains of their dummy practice torpedoes.

seventy men. You can be very good, as an individual, at moving a submarine from A to B, you can handle it dived quite competently, but unless you can actually take seventy men with you and have them work for you, and have them enjoy it, then you really don't have the qualities that are necessary to command.'

As the course progresses, it is these intangible qualities of command that Evans is beginning to search for, as well as the sheer ability to carry out well-executed attacks. It is also, in a different way, what the crew of HMS *Oracle* is looking for. They have absolutely no influence on the decision that Evans must make about who will pass or who will fail, but the way in which they react to the students in the control room must be some kind of pointer for Evans.

As the days pass by, and the complexity of the attacks increases as the numbers of frigates involved rises from one to two to three, it becomes apparent in the control room that some students have a better rapport with the crew than others. It is a difficult change to pinpoint. It is not as if anyone is reluctant to do his job properly – no one would dare – but occasionally there is just that little bit less eagerness in their manner, less anticipation perhaps; a feeling that they are not being carried along.

One habit that all the students have difficulty throwing off is getting so obsessed with looking through the periscope that they forget what else is happening in the control room. It is a ritual of submarine routine that all orders from the Captain are instantly repeated by the person to whom the order is addressed, as an acknowledgement that he has heard and understood the order. Then, as soon as that order has been executed, he will announce that fact to the captain, who in turn is expected to acknowledge it. Thus, for instance, when diving to ninety feet from periscope depth the captain will give the command 'Lower all masts'. (It is important that both periscopes, the wireless mast and the radar mast should be lowered if a frigate is about to thunder past fifteen feet overhead.) The hoist operator will then repeat 'Lower all masts', lower them, and a few seconds later will call out 'All masts fully lowered' – to which the captain should reply 'Roger all masts fully lowered'. Crash diving to ninety feet is a tense time in the Perisher, and the student will be concentrating on stopwatches, sonar reports and the depth gauge – and as a result will often fail to acknowledge the shout from the hoist operator. Evans would pounce on this, and tell the operator to repeat his call – but still the student would not hear. Finally the operator would have literally to shout out 'ALL MASTS FULLY LOWERED' – whereupon the Perisher would sheepishly acknowledge the report. One of the worst offenders at this selective deafness is Simon Bebbington. So one day

Evans decides to make the point once and for all. As Simon's attack starts, and he becomes engrossed in ranging on the periscope, Evans signals to George Webster, the submarine's real captain, to start distributing ear defenders around the control room. These are large, yellow headphones, used to protect the eardrums of the engineers who work alongside the diesels. Slowly and surreptitiously everyone in the control room puts them on: Simon's periscope assistant, the planesman, the First Lieutenant who executes depth and engine-speed changes, the 'Q' panel operator, everyone in sight – even Teacher himself. Simon blithely continues with his attack, absolutely unaware of the practical joke that is being played on him. Evans even keeps remarking, 'Speak up, Captain, I can't hear you,' but still Simon continues, engrossed in his attack – and blind to his crew. Finally, well after moving over to the First Lieutenant and the planesman to study their instruments, he suddenly realises what is happening – and irritably tells the First Lieutenant to 'take those damn things off your ears'. But, as he later acknowledges with a rueful smile, the point has been made and he is grateful it has been done in a relatively mild way.

'I should have noticed at an earlier stage than when I did. It's to test our awareness of what's going on around us. It's also meant to break concentration to see whether you can keep the rhythm of the attack going.' In the past I've seen people barging through the control room with fire hoses – or a chef coming screaming from the galley pretending he's cut his finger off. Last year I even saw someone come in with a case of beer, drop it all over the deck, and then open a tin and spray everyone with it.

Other students reveal their excessive concentration on the periscope in different ways. Gavin McClaren, for instance, once pressed his eye so hard against the eyepiece in a frenzy of range-finding that he cut his eyebrow. Blood trickled down his face for the rest of the attack – but he didn't notice until it was all over. Overconcentration on the periscope is one sign that the student is not sufficiently conscious of his crew – overimpatience is another. Tiny Lister's huge bulk is an inherent problem for him in a cramped diesel submarine. As more and more ships join the attacks, the students must continually pan from one frigate to another, which means they must pull the periscope quickly through 180° and swing around with it. Increasingly, Lister's bulky backside bumps into one or other of the ratings standing close by, despite their best efforts to keep out of the way. Bumping into people on submarines is an accepted hazard – almost a way of life – and normally it bothers no one. But Lister becomes easily irritated by it and starts shouting at everyone to keep out of his way, even though they are already doing their best to do so. Momentary flickers of resentment start to cross the unfortunate ratings' faces.

At the end of the second week at sea, the students are now facing three frigates simultaneously, as well as the normal complement of fishing boats. Attacks climax in a maelstrom of activity, since as often as not two of the frigates will skirt either side of the go-deep circle, with the third charging straight towards the submarine. The frigates are performing well, keeping their course so accurately that the students are in a constant torment of doubt about whether or not to play safe and go deep. They make mistakes – and still several times each day Dai Evans has to step in and flood 'Q' ('five very friendly tons', as he describes the contents of the tank) in order to save the submarine from collision. But every time he has to do this is another black mark for the student concerned.

It is an extremely testing time for the Perisher. By now Teacher expects them to be fully capable of dealing with such situations, and any errors they make, particularly on safety, are critical. As each student collapses into the goatshed after his attack, he reflects on the attack he's just carried out – and his progress in general.

David Charlton: 'That felt quite nice – it went smoothly until the end when I went deep a little too early because of the right-wing escort.' Charlton still speaks so quickly that it can be hard to follow his words; but the hesitancy which used to look like a symptom of lack of confidence now appears as a polite concern for everyone's well-being. 'The big change was from one ship to two ships – having to put each one on a separate stopwatch and so on. The change from two to three didn't seem so difficult.' Charlton's hesitancy becomes very diplomatic when asked about his progress in Perisher. 'I don't seem to be worse or better than anyone else – but from the comments that Teacher makes, I certainly hope I'm still in with a chance. I don't like to consider the question of passing or failing – it's just putting an unnecessary strain on yourself. I'm enjoying myself – driving a submarine around with three frigates coming pretty close, and still remaining safe – there's quite a lot of satisfaction in that.'

In contrast to Charlton's emerging quiet confidence, Gavin McClaren slumps into the goatshed with a sigh and a sad shake of the head, feeling for his cigarettes. He has just had a bad attack – not an unsafe one, but quite the opposite. Distracted by a nearby fishing boat, he miscalculated the position of the escorts and went deep unnecessarily, right at the beginning of the attack, thus wasting the entire run. 'I've had several like that – but not for some days. It's irritating, annoying. The fishing vessel threw me – he was only 1000 yards away, ahead of us, so we were closing him. I went through a bad confidence thing last week, but it's been getting better – yesterday was good. Now I've done two bad ones today. It's a worry to be doing that sort of thing at this stage in the course.

'I don't really know how I'm doing overall. It's very hard to tell because one is not absolutely certain what is being looked for. We all know you have to be safe, and if you're not you won't get through this particular part of the course – but if you are safe, you're not automatically going to get through. It's a question of what other things Teacher is looking for – awareness of what's going on on the surface, command presence, control of the team. He assesses you in everything – the way you deal with the ship's company, the way you deal with him. But safety is always first. So I don't know, I really don't. Some days I think I'm doing pretty well, other days I think – this is dreadful, I'll never make it. You do think about failure. Not during the day, but in the evening perhaps, or when you first wake up in the morning. It's worrying, and I think that anybody who claims he doesn't think about failure isn't telling the truth. You don't talk about it, and you try not to think about it – certainly during the actual attacks.'

Gavin disappears back to the control room and Tiny Lister squeezes into the goatshed in his place. Lister too has had a bad attack. He was forced deep by the third ship and executed that manoeuvre satisfactorily. However, some kind of mistake was made on the ranges of the two other escorts, and the result was that Lister decided to bring the submarine back to periscope depth when it was still theoretically unsafe to do so. Dai Evans had to step in, take command of the submarine, and contradict Lister's orders to return to periscope depth. Lister is convinced that the mistake in ranges was not his own, that the information fed back to him did not match his original estimate. 'I suppose it's a black mark against me. I'm extremely annoyed about it. I'm pretty certain that if I'd been given the right range I wouldn't have come up, but there's not much time to do all these things. If you get hold of the wrong information, you make the wrong decision.'

As he speaks the next attack is already in full swing. The submarine tilts perceptibly downwards as it goes into the 'Q' routine. 'In general it's been pretty patchy – not as good as I'd hoped. Things have picked up in the last few days – I've been working pretty hard at it. The last two attacks I did went pretty well, but with this one I really got shot down in a shower of flames at the end.'

As he finishes, a slithering, sliding noise marks the passage of 3000 tons of frigate just a few feet above our heads. Tiny barely notices it without prompting. 'Yes, you could hear the rotation of the propellers. To somebody from outside, a newcomer, it must seem horrifying seeing a ship thundering in through the periscope. But once you've done it a few times, it's quite normal.'

A student can be failed at any time on the Perisher course, but the end of this first period at sea – now just seven days away – is a major decision point for Teacher. By then he must make up his mind whether or not the student is safe – the basic criterion for him continuing on the course. Dai Evans is satisfied with the progress of two of the students, a little concerned about the third, and increasingly anxious about the fourth. At the end of the afternoon, each of them is called into the Captain's cabin for a progress report from Teacher. One by one they come in, concerned, preoccupied young faces next to the tired but calm Teacher. Squashed close together on the tiny seat, under constant observation in a cramped submarine, there's no room to hide fears, conceal deficiencies in technique, or pretend your mood is other than it is. First is McClaren. Evans chooses his words with care; he knows that each student will remember every one.

'OK Gavin, it's the end of the second week, there's just a week to go – so I wanted to tell you how you were getting on. At the end of the attack-teacher time your progress was good, and you came to sea well prepared. Your progress since then has been steadily upwards, although there have been some thorny patches in it, and those, I think, are due to lack of thought at the time rather than an inability to do it. The handling of fishing boats particularly, and the length of time between all-round looks.' Gavin nods quietly in agreement to Teacher's remarks. He appears the most tired of all students, with patches of dark grey under his deep-set, red-rimmed eyes. '. . . You've got the ability to do it, I'm sure of that – but you've got to demonstrate to me that you *can* do it. OK, happy?'

'Yes, sir, I'd agree with all that. I'm just starting to enjoy it, actually; I was hoping to get another attack in today.'

'OK, well – the next attack is always the best, right?'

Gavin is replaced by David Charlton.

'. . . You've done some very neat attacks – you occasionally make mistakes, but I see nothing in your performance that I'm worried about. The attacks will be a little harder next week – the ships will be going a little faster, and there'll be a fourth frigate from Wednesday – but I don't think that should worry you. . . .'

Charlton can only agree with this praise; it is remarkable how much he has gained in confidence and stature since the beginning of the course. Despite his quiet manner, he is beginning to exude the kind of authority that Evans is looking for.

Next is Simon Bebbington. 'I think you already feel comfortable, you know what you want to achieve. You've done some very neat attacks, you've got the ship's company behind you, supporting you in the control room. You make mistakes, and you will continue to make mistakes next week, but they are of a very minor nature. What I want to see you do next week is aim for some polish, because I think you've reached the stage where you're able to do that.'

Last is Tiny. '. . . At the end of the attack-teacher time your progress was satisfactory, and since then there's no doubt in my mind that you have come on – but although the peaks have been good, the troughs are the problem. You must try to get rid of them. When you have a bad attack, put it behind you and come into the next attack determined that that is going to be the best one. At the beginning of the attack, set everything up in the right way so that you can recognise the disposition of the force coming towards you – and any other threat around – and then take action to deal with it. When you have done all that, then your attacks have been good, but when you don't think about the problem fully, that's when you hit the troughs – and I am concerned about the rate at which you're hitting them. You've shown me what you can do, but you must show me that you can sustain that performance all the time. When you're in command, you can't afford to have an off day, because the buck stops with you. OK?'

Lister has been pensively looking down at his notes during Evans' talk. He is beginning to have the hunted look of someone who knows that he is just slightly out of his depth, but is nevertheless striving to conquer the problem. He concedes that everything Teacher has said is valid, and leaves.

Evans sits on, alone. He knows that in the next week he will be faced with the one aspect of the Perisher that he dreads: the possibility of having to fail a student.

That same evening, the students follow the tradition of the Perisher course, and throw a mess dinner in the Douglas Hotel to which they invite the officers of the two submarines. It is a formal occasion, which marks their gratitude for the help they have received over the past two weeks, and which they will continue to receive during the coming months. The timing within the course is interesting. With less than half their submarine-based time elapsed, it seems a little premature to be saying thank you to the officers; however, it could be that this is the last Friday that all the students will still be together on the course.

HMS *Oberon* diving with the slim attack periscope raised.

The hotel's dining room is entirely rearranged so that the tables form a large square; special menus are printed, entitled 'Perisher Dinner', and extra waitresses wait apprehensively for the invasion. Downstairs in the Perisher Bar, the course and their guests are marshalled into order at exactly one minute to eight by the senior student – Lt Cdr Tiny Lister. He leads the way up the stairs, and in the hall a lone piper starts playing. The piper takes over the head of the procession and leads on into the dining room, where he stands and continues his lament as first Lister, then the remainder of the procession, file in. Of all ten students on the two halves of the course, Lister is at this moment the most likely to be absent by the following Friday night. He probably knows that himself, and it seems a cruel irony that the extra pressure of leading the dinner and having to make a speech should fall on his broad but heavily-burdened shoulders. However, he manages well with the speech, making jokes at his own expense about size and weight. Later there are songs, some dancing and many drunken conversations and confessions. It is well into the early morning before everyone is asleep.

The procedure for failing a Perisher student follows a set pattern. On the Wednesday evening of the last week of this first sea period, the two Teachers meet to discuss their students. If one of them feels he has a potential failure in his group, he talks it through with his colleague and, if they agree that the student may have to go, they telephone Faslane to initiate the complex arrangements necessary. It is felt that because of the extreme effects on an officer and on his career of leaving the Perisher the break should be as quick, clean and delicately handled as possible. The final decision will be made by the Teacher on the submarine on Thursday, after the suspect student has been given some final attack runs in which to prove himself. A waiting launch will rendezvous with the submarine, take the failed Perisher off, accompanied by Teacher's Petty Officer Steward and a bottle of whisky from the hotel, and return him to Arran while the other students are still at sea. Before they return he will have packed his bags and been whisked back to Faslane. And there he'll be met by a sympathetic senior officer, dispatched straight home by train or plane for two weeks' holiday, and to all intents and purposes consigned to oblivion. Stories of breakdowns and tears from students when told of their failure are legion.

By Wednesday morning Dai Evans has become noticeably withdrawn and quiet. He still does all the teaching and operational work required in the control room, but he is unusually quiet in the wardroom at mealtimes; his depression almost makes it seem that he is the one who is in danger of failing. In fact he admits that he does feel he has failed if a student does not make it.

The cause of his anxiety is Tiny Lister, who has not managed to get rid of those troughs of bad attacks. His problem is partly that he cannot get into the right rhythm. He is too often unsure of the layout of the groups of surface ships heading towards him; he cannot paint a full mental picture of their positions, relative to his own and to each other. He is therefore never quite on top of things; he is constantly taken by surprise, constantly having to make up for lost time, constantly just slightly disorganised. He knows it, and he knows that the moment of truth is not far away. It may be for this reason that he is becoming more aggressive in the control room, more deeply sunk in thought away from it. Woe betide anyone who gets in his way now during an attack; a bellow of 'Get out of my way' bursts forth. During one particularly difficult attack the submarine's trim is bad and the depth increases by two or three feet – just enough to dip the periscope head in the water with every other wave and blind the student for a few seconds as the water drains. Lister starts roaring at the planesman to keep the submarine on depth, but HMS *Oracle* proves difficult to trim that morning and he keeps getting blinded. Finally, to show support and vent his own feelings, Teacher roars into action too, issuing dire threats about what he will do to the depth-keeper if he doesn't get the submarine on depth.

The aggression and the lack of finesse in Lister's attacks wouldn't matter if he were safe – if he unfailingly went to ninety feet every time his go-deep circle was penetrated. But he doesn't. Still, after three weeks at sea, he either cannot calculate the ranges sufficiently quickly and accurately, or he cannot understand when a frigate has turned to charge towards him. Time and again Evans allows the frigate to come 100 yards or even 200 yards inside the circle, soaking up the safety margin, before taking over from Lister and flooding 'Q' tank to send HMS *Oracle* sliding sharply downwards. Every time he does so, the stopwatches check how many seconds elapse before the extra-ordinary rattling, squealing sound of the frigate passes directly overhead. Invariably it's less than the required sixty seconds, confirming that Teacher did not 'Q' the submarine prematurely – but that Tiny failed to do it on time.

On Wednesday evening the two Teachers meet for their last discussion on this first period of Perisher. Bob Stevens, like Evans, is looking much more tired and drawn than just three weeks ago; the laugh lines around his eyes have deepened and multiplied under the strain of ensuring twenty times every day that HMS *Otter* is not about to be rammed. He confirms to Evans that, of his five students, four are certain to pass this first part of Perisher, but the fifth is a little doubtful. Mike Washer's technical ability is satisfactory, but he tends to crack under pressure. 'He starts garbling his orders, rushing around – he finds anything to do which will keep him occupied as opposed to actually stepping back from it all and getting a feel of what the problem is. He overlooks desperately. I shouted at him in the control room today for that. I told him once, don't overlook, twice, don't overlook, and the third time I just lost my cool and blasted him. He's so terribly uptight as a Perisher. If only he'd lose his nervousness I feel he'd come through it. But I can't be sure – so tomorrow I'm going to put him under pressure. I'll give them one attack each, and then Mike will go on and on until I'm convinced he can handle it.'

Dai Evans listens carefully, recognising that Stevens has some of the same problems as himself. 'Simon is there – he's got it completely. David Charlton is very close behind. Gavin I was a little bit concerned about, but he had one attack today which was outstanding – he didn't put a foot wrong, so I reckon that as long as he has a good day tomorrow, he'll be OK.' Dai pauses, reflects, takes a deep breath and continues. 'Tiny, on the other hand, continues to make mistakes which have no pattern to them. Under extreme stress he alienates himself from the team – he told his periscope assistant today, 'Get out of my bloody way.' He was very quiet tonight. I Q'd him twice today – I let the frigate come to about 950 yards before I took over. If he has a good day tomorrow, I'll take him through to the next period; if he doesn't then he'll go. My inclination at the moment is fifty-five per cent against him passing. The other thing I've found is that he can't shrug off a bad attack – and if he were to be in command, that's something he'd have to do.'

Bob nods, and thinks back to the day in the previous week, when the two Teachers had swopped submarines, to give each of them a perspective on the other half of the course. 'For what it's worth, when I rode with your lot Tiny had four attacks. I've got a pretty straight idea about what's dangerous; and all four were dangerous.'

The tension amongst the students that night is high. They all know that the following day, the penultimate of this part of the course, is the day on which failures will be told the bad news – although, just to keep the successful ones on tenterhooks, *they* won't be told that they are through until the Friday. The bar is unusually empty; as I walk to my room after dinner a voice, speaking so softly into the telephone that it is unidentifiable, floats out from a bedroom whose door has been left ajar. '. . . Don't worry, darling. By this time tomorrow it'll be all over – either I'll be home or I'll be through.'

Thursday 6 October dawns grey and cold. A subdued Perisher and an unusually brusque Teacher clamber on board HMS *Oracle*. The submarine slips its moorings and, under the command of Lt Cdr Tiny Lister, heads out to sea. The crew also know that today is the day of reckoning. They have been keeping a book on who will pass for the past three weeks, and their odds match Teacher's closely. The most subdued rating on board is Petty Officer Finch. 'Chirpy' is Dai Evans' and the Perisher's steward, which not only means that he keeps them supplied with coffee and cigarettes, but also that he makes all travel arrangements and is Evans' personal assistant. In the Navy for over twenty years since his mid-teens, Chirpy professes great devotion to 'my boys'. He knows that he may today have the difficult job of comforting and accompanying a failure, and he has acquired a bottle of whisky as an aid – which, for the moment, he keeps well hidden. Nothing is decided – so the preparation for failure must be kept invisible to the students.

Today, as yesterday, there are four frigates attacking the submarine simultaneously, at high speed. Three come in a broad first wave, with the fourth just behind. For a student who is on top of his technique this represents a challenge which is actually quite enjoyable. It is an artificial situation – and one that he is unlikely to face again in his career – but one that he will look back on with nostalgia for years to come. These last days of attacks represent the rewards for all the hard work of the past weeks. Up to now even the most proficient students have been constantly struggling to keep abreast of the developments, as the numbers of ships and their speeds have increased. Now they should have reached the crest of the wave and be coasting down the other side.

For Simon and David, this is the case: they enter the control room exuding authority, and handle their attacks with aplomb. Gavin may not enjoy them so much, but he has no real problems and handles the submarine competently. But Tiny is still inconsistent. From mid-morning Evans stops the normal rotation of attacks and makes Tiny continue to do run after run. It is his last opportunity to prove himself, but try as he might, he still cannot conquer his aggression, inconsistency and sheer mistakes. The atmosphere in the submarine becomes progressively more tense until, quite suddenly, several things happen at once.

At the end of Tiny's latest attack, instead of turning and preparing for the next one the submarine is ordered to surface – not by Tiny, but by HMS *Oracle*'s resident captain, George Webster. When the Perisher are on board Webster normally takes a back seat – except when specifically asked to take over by Teacher.

As the high-pressure air hisses into the submarine's ballast tanks, and HMS *Oracle* rises through the surface of the Clyde, Dai Evans sits quietly in the Captain's cabin. Finally he gets up, carefully puts on his tie, and strides out through the control room. His face set, he calls down the passageway to Chirpy, 'Petty Officer Finch – would you ask Lt Cdr Lister to come to my cabin, please?' Lister, knowing what is about to come, walks through the busy control room – his eyes straight ahead, everyone else's avoiding his glance. Back by the wardroom, the one absolutely sure sign of failure is there for all to see – Chirpy is putting on a heavy sweater and raincoat. This can only mean one thing – that he is about to leave the submarine, and that he will not be alone.

Five minutes later, Lister, Evans and Finch troop forrard down the submarine to the main access hatch, climb up the ladder in grim-faced silence, and depart. The tender is already waiting alongside. Teacher and student shake hands, and, accompanied by Chirpy, the ex-engineer jumps across the narrow gap between the brown-painted tender and the black, rounded hull of the submarine. It is quite possibly the last time Lister will ever set foot on a submarine.

'I had to fail Tiny because of his inconsistency. He was marvellous about it – he took it with tremendous dignity. It's a day I loathe, because it's a decision that means he will never go back to being in submarines. I wish everyone knew the sort of pressures that a Perisher student actually goes through on this course, whether he passes or fails.'

A few days later, Lister decides with the Naval Careers office that he should take the traditional escape route for failed Perishers and move into the surface Navy. General service, it is officially called; submariners disparagingly call it the Grey Funnel line. He will train to be a Principal Warfare Officer – a job in which he will benefit from his submarine experience and which might lead to command of a surface vessel. Later sitting in his town house in Portsmouth, he is philosophical as he thinks back to that difficult afternoon.

'I must say that during the three consecutive attacks I'd felt that I hadn't really made the grade. So it was something less than a surprise when Teacher called me to his cabin to tell me I'd failed. It helped that I'd already come to the same conclusion – in fact, in the end it was something of a relief. He told me what the routine would be for taking me off the submarine, and then he poured me a stiff whisky, and we chatted about the next stage in my career. Some people I know take it very badly, especially if they consider that they were up to standard. It took two or three days before I really realised what had happened. I think I'll always be disappointed. I would have loved to pass the course – I would have been thrilled to get a job commanding a submarine. But I must accept that it won't happen, and I only hope I will enjoy the next stage in my career as much as I've enjoyed being in the submarine service. I'm sure I will.'

The day after Tiny leaves, Gavin, Simon and David are told by Teacher that they have passed the first part of the course. In a typically restrained scene the obviously delighted Evans conveys the good news to the three students in as few words as possible – and they in turn do their best to repress their feelings. A bottle of champagne in the goatshed does little to loosen them up.

Gavin: I'm suddenly realising how tired I feel. I'm absolutely shattered – and there's the next phase coming up, too.

David: The pleasure is tinged with having lost Tiny. It's surprising how close you get as a team.

Simon: I think everybody realised he wasn't finding it as easy as he should have been. He was fairly cheerful last night and I think he was relieved that it was soon going to be over.

They all praise Dai Evans' role in their own successes and acknowledge that he too is sad about losing Tiny. 'His commitment to getting us through is total, and he was very upset when Tiny went. But he's delighted we've hung on – he's that committed to it. We owe him a lot and undoubtedly we'll owe him a lot more by the end.'

The truth is that the three remaining Perishers were less shocked by the departure of one of their brethren than might normally be expected: partly because it had been expected for some time, partly because Tiny, as an ex-engineer, had never quite shared the rapport that the other three enjoyed. David Charlton, Gavin McClaren and Simon Bebbington were clearly undergoing the kind of experience that creates deep and lasting friendships. David and Gavin had been close friends anyway, but all three were now beginning to be surrounded by an invisible web of companionship that both bound them together and kept them slightly apart from everyone else on board.

As the three sipped their champagne, they reflected that despite the achievement of the past few weeks and despite the exhaustion they already felt, they were still only half-way through the course. Ahead lay several more weeks of lecture-room and simulator work, followed by another three-week period at sea which would be at least as testing as that which had just finished.

On the other half of the course, Bob Stevens had decided that his only doubtful candidate was good enough to continue the course.

So now there were eight. . . .

For the next three weeks the students go back into the classroom and into the simulator. Now they are learning quite different skills. Their submarine handling and safety techniques are proven; the artificially orchestrated attacks of the first part of the course are redundant. Now they progress to learning the real business of submarine tactics.

Much of a modern submarine's work is covert. The whole value of these craft is that they can remain invisible; and their operational tasks and tactics are based on preserving and exploiting that precious asset. Polaris submarines must remain undetected in order to preserve the value of the deterrent they carry. They are probably the most successful of all types of Royal Navy submarines at keeping invisible; but they do this largely by travelling extremely slowly and deliberately avoiding contact with any other submarine; essentially by remaining passive. Nuclear-powered hunter-killer submarines such as *Warspite* have a more active role, but they have one

HMS *Oberon* (*above*) showing the conventional bow shape of the
diesel-electric submarine, and HMS *Olympus* (*below*) benefiting from its
protection in the open ocean.

disadvantage compared with diesel-electric submarines: their large size and deep draught makes it impossible for them to operate in shallow water. The diesel-electrics can quietly and carefully inch their way very close to coastlines, which makes them invaluable for at least three of the submarine's most important tasks – photography, mine-laying, and the transfer of personnel either to or from a hostile country.

It is these operations, as well as work with anti-submarine-warfare frigates and aircraft, that form the basis of the second part of the Perisher. The students are now learning to be commanding officers in as complete a way as possible. They take command of the submarine not for twenty minutes at a time, but for up to twenty-four hours. They plan complete operations, brief the ship's company, execute the plan – modifying it if necessary as it unfolds. There are far fewer hard-and-fast rules to abide by. Teacher is looking for resourcefulness, imagination and adaptability as much as a display of learned technique. The students must also show that they can cope with all the internal running of a submarine, and that they can control, lead and occasionally inspire the ship's company. Broken limbs, broken equipment, personnel problems – usually real, sometimes deliberately faked by Teacher – all of these test the student's capacity to command.

On the evening of 24 November HMS *Oracle* is due to carry out an agent rendezvous with a naval tender. The fact that the agent in question is actually a BBC film crew is beside the point; the operation must still be carried out as if for real. The Firth of Clyde is whipped into a vicious swell, and the tender pitches uncomfortably. As we approach the rendezvous area the skipper shuts off all the lights and starts a prearranged cycle of turning the engine off and on at one-minute intervals, hoping that this pattern will be picked up on the waiting submarine's sonar. His face, lit only by the green glow from the radar screen, glances anxiously back and forth between the inky night and the screen, searching for any other vessels. We know that there is likely to be a frigate in the area, like us without lights, searching for the submarine. There are fishing boats about, too, but they are easy to see with their bright white lights.

The skipper gives a muffled exclamation as he looks at the screen. He has identified a blip that he reckons is the frigate. We have reached the rendezvous point, but the submarine will not dare to surface while the frigate is so close, so we must wait, stopped and silent. Later, a ghostly grey shape slides silently past, slows down uncertainly, turns, and slips away again. He is looking for *Oracle* – but presumably he has not found her. Ten minutes later the radio crackles into life. *Oracle* has come to periscope depth, raised her wireless mast, but is unable to pick us out from the several fishing boats close by. We flash our masthead light three times – then again, and again. It is becoming rather a public clandestine rendezvous, but finally they spot us and surface. We move quietly towards the near-invisible shape of the submarine, across a suddenly calm Clyde. A scramble across to the wet casing, red torches showing the way down the hatch, and the transfer is complete.

The inside of the submarine is in the most contradictory of conditions, black light. The inky gloom means not even the dim red fluorescents are on. The only light is from instruments or heavily-shaded red torches. The gloom makes it even more cramped than usual – people and projections keep materialising from everywhere and bumping the unfortunate newcomer. The stuffy atmosphere betrays a lengthy period just spent under the sea. As soon as the hatches are closed, normal lighting is switched on at either end of the submarine and it is possible to move around. But the central section remains in black light, to allow periscope-watchkeepers' pupils to expand as much as possible. Double layers of heavy black curtains at either end of the control room provide a barrier against white light.

Peering through the gloom, it is possible to recognise faces. Teacher is there, and Simon and David. But there is one missing. Gavin is nowhere to be seen. He left the submarine twenty-four hours earlier.

And then there were seven. . . .

One week earlier, the submarine was heading towards coastal waters after two weeks of deep-sea work. Gavin McClaren had done well on this part of the course, and his confidence was high. But the move to inshore waters meant the return of his old bugbear, the fishing boats. He had had difficulty coping with these during the first period at sea, but had conquered the problem sufficiently to pull himself through. But now they had returned he suddenly found his self-confidence – at the best of times a fragile shell – beginning to crack again. Every time he became involved in operations where a major threat, such as a frigate, was accompanied by the peripheral problem of fishing boats, Gavin became more and more worried. Although he knew exactly what to do about them – to establish where they were, how much of a safety threat they represented, and then to ignore them for a while and concentrate on the main threat – he found he simply could not get them out of his mind, could not concentrate on the point of the operation. As he put it several weeks later, 'It was a question of not being able to rub my stomach and pat my head at the same time. A

The ratings' bunkspace on *Warspite*: 40 men sleep in an area the size of the average garage, three bunks high on either side of a narrow passageway.

The biggest single space on *Warspite* is the fore-ends. A rating exercises amongst the Sub-Harpoon missiles and torpedo tubes.

HMS *Walrus*, a diesel-electric submarine of the Porpoise class. Designed in the 1950s, the few remaining P-class boats are approaching the end of their operational life. Note the folded foreplanes, which will be lowered to the horizontal position for diving.

HMS *Otter*, a sister submarine to the Perisher's HMS *Oracle*. One of the Royal Navy's thirteen O-class diesel-electric submarines, it is capable of 15 knots underwater. It displaces 2410 tons when submerged, is 295 feet long, and has a crew of seven officers and 62 ratings.

Left The Captain at the attack periscope on HMS *Warspite*.

The Douglas Hotel, Arran, where the Perishers stay for part of their course.

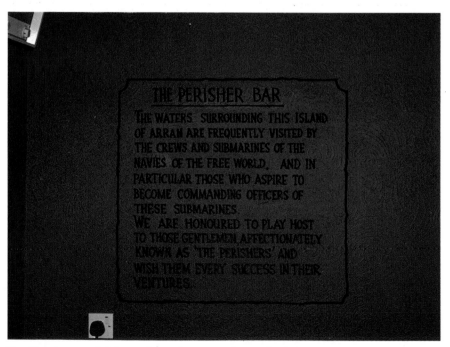

Dedication to visiting submariners on the wall of the Perisher bar in the Douglas Hotel.

Cdr Bob Stevens and Cdr Dai Evans in the Perisher bar.

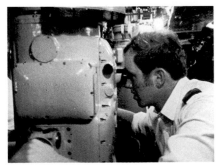

In the control room of HMS *Oracle*   *Left* Lt Cdr Gavin McClaren and Cdr Dai Evans. *Right* Lt David Charlton checking a range.

Sergeant Ezra Lee making his escape in Bushnell's 'Turtle'.

Fulton's *Nautilus*, with sail raised for surface running.

Early submarines had petrol engines, and the inflammable vapour could have disastrous results. Several lives were lost when A5 suffered an explosion in 1905.

A commemorative poster of the sinking of the *Lusitania*. It includes facsimiles of a commemorative medal issued in Germany; one side shows a skeleton issuing tickets at the Cunard office in New York, presumably representing the company's disregard for Germany's warnings; the other shows the liner sinking with the heavily ironic words 'No Contraband'.

The artist Felix Schwormstadt provided a glamourised image of U-boats during World War I. It is unlikely that crews bothered to wear hats in the control room (top), and rescuing of merchant-ship crews was confined to the early months of the war.

question of not being able to control my mind sufficiently, to keep my imagination under control. I couldn't put the fishing boats into a separate compartment in my mind and get on with the rest of the business.'

Slowly the awful truth began to dawn on Gavin that he might never be able to conquer this particular problem. His confidence slipped away faster and faster; he became physically ill and had to spend a day in bed, his mind constantly revolving around the fishing boats. The next day, Monday 21 November, he felt better and resumed his duties. He was due to carry out an intelligence-gathering exercise against a frigate in the Clyde. This neccessarily involved keeping the periscope down as much as possible, for fear of detection. The technique is to raise the periscope briefly, take the necessary ranges and bearings on whatever is in sight, and then lower it, plot their positions, and think carefully about what to do next and whether the fishing boats are going to prove a problem. But, unfortunately, Gavin just couldn't stop himself from worrying. 'The fishing boats began to panic me. I couldn't concentrate on anything else except these blasted fishing boats.'

In a blinding flash Gavin realised that he would never be able to conquer this mental blockage – that he would always be wanting to take extra, unnecessary looks at fishing boats – and that as a submarine captain his judgement would be compromised by this fear in his imagination. 'About 11.30 that morning I said to Teacher, "I must have a word with you." We went to his cabin, he sat me down and I told him I had this problem. It was difficult to explain – he's done the course, passed it and commanded two submarines, so it's not a problem that he has. It was all a bit emotional. After all, I was failing a course which I'd been aiming to do for the past ten years. So it wasn't a very happy fifteen minutes. We agreed there and then that it would be the end of the course for me.'

Gavin stayed in the cabin, shattered, while Dai went to arrange his departure. In the usual dramatic manner of the Perisher, the failed student was lifted off the submarine by helicopter at 5.30 that same afternoon. Evans remains uncommunicative about Gavin's failure. 'Unfortunately Gavin realised that his ability was not up to it. He realised that himself – it didn't need me to tell him that he couldn't do it. It's just very sad when that happens. He is bitterly disappointed – it's not a nice experience.'

It is possible that Dai was taken by surprise at the suddenness of Gavin's decision. Yet he must have been relieved that he did not have to take the initiative with the news of failure. Perhaps the most important point is the near-exhaustion that is enveloping Evans has forced him to cut his mind off from the failure of the recent past, to allow full concentration on the problems of the present.

It is very hard to judge exactly why Gavin McClaren failed the Perisher. Clearly he had a genuine problem with fishing boats; this was apparent throughout the course. But that inability to control his mind and imagination may have been a symptom of a fundamental lack of belief in his own capabilities. Throughout the course he was the most overtly nervous of the students – even the struggling Tiny Lister had a calmer, more philosophical approach to his problems – and right from the start of the course he was intrigued by the qualities others possessed, and he needed, to command a submarine. Maybe he just did not have those qualities, and it took the Perisher course to make that apparent. Maybe he was an example of Sandy Woodward's earlier remarks, predicting the stress the students would be put under: 'We need to know your limitations . . . and it's an opportunity for you to find yourselves.' The stress of the Perisher made Gavin McClaren dig sufficiently deeply into his soul and mind to discover that he did not quite have the right qualities for command.

Three weeks later, he is putting a brave face on his failure. McClaren lives on a small sailing yacht in Dumbarton; the boat provides him with a consuming interest. In the tiny but neat cabin, reminiscent in its cramped orderliness of a submarine, he proudly shows scrapbooks full of photographs of voyages around the coast of Scotland, the neat diagrams and diaries betraying the professional background. He has started a beard, his deep-set eyes seem to have sunk even further into their sockets; despite his brave attempts at being positive, he is clearly a deeply disappointed man.

'I made a positive decision in the helicopter that I wouldn't let it get me down. I feel a *sense* of failure, but I don't actually feel "a failure". To spend the whole of one's naval career aiming at this course, and to fail at the last minute – it was a great disappointment. But there are other things I can do, and other things that are important to me, like this boat. My other interests lessened the shock a bit.'

McClaren has decided to try and avoid the traditional route of the failed Perisher. Instead of going to join surface warships he will remain in the Submarine Service, albeit in a shore job. The only opportunity he will have to go to sea in a submarine will be as a 'rider' – a short-term visitor. Already he is beginning to experience the stigma of the failed Perisher. 'People don't know what to say to you. It's like coming across someone who's just had a bereavement in the family – do you mention it, do you let it drop, do you bring it out into the open? People aren't sure how to play it because they don't see many people who've failed Perisher. Yes of course I'd have loved to have passed and commanded a submarine – but you can't do everything. I would have loved to have done it, but it's not to be. Rather like people who have three daughters and say, "I'd have liked a son". Well, not everybody has sons. That sort of feeling, I think.'

Back on HMS *Oracle* the remaining students and Teacher, and indeed most of the crew, look extraordinarily tired. Dai Evans has sprouted the beginnings of a beard, there are pronounced black circles around his eyes, and his face is grey with fatigue. But his commitment to the course is as strong as ever – and it's become competitive. For the past 2½ weeks *Oracle* has effectively been at war – albeit against a token force of one or two frigates and the occasional aircraft – and Evans is hugely satisfied that, as far as he can tell, the submarine has come out on top of what has been an exhausting game of cat and mouse. Despite his increasingly scruffy appearance, Evans seems even more alert and excited by the sheer involvement of the course than ever.

Simon Bebbington and David Charlton are wondering when the adrenalin will run out. When Tiny left at the end of the first sea period, there was talk about the possibility of moving one student from the other half of the course across to *Oracle* to balance up the numbers – because it was felt that to have only three students would place an undue strain on them. But it did not happen; it would have been difficult for a new face to have been absorbed into that close-knit trio.

Now, with just two students left, the pressure is intense. The submarine's workload is high, and their different tasks follow straight on from one to the next. Each student takes it in turn to command the submarine, for periods of up to twelve hours at a time. Whichever student is not in command must usually act as his captain's right-hand man in the control room, or plan ahead to whatever task he has to do next with the submarine. Sleep comes a poor third.

The ship's company is getting tired too. Perisher-running is an extremely busy time for them. It also brings extra people on to an already cramped submarine. Students and Teacher are all highly motivated, and will put up with anything for the sake of success, but to the average rating in the control room Perisher means several new chiefs, some of whom are not too sure about the orders they give to the Indians.

For the remaining two days of the course, the submarine will stay in this area, doing three different kinds of tasks. The first is laying mines. This has traditionally been one of the submarine's most useful roles, and for the student is principally an exercise in precision navigation. The area to be sown with mines is the Cumbrae Gap, a narrow stretch of water between Little Cumbrae Island to the east and the southermost point of the Island of Bute to the west. It is the entrance to the Port of Glasgow, and to the major submarine base at Faslane – and so it is a possible target for mine-laying in the event of any real conflict.

It is Simon's turn to take command for this exercise; he has already planned his tactics and has to brief the rest of the submarine's officers in the wardroom. Action Stations are called and the control room fills with people. But what follows is quite unlike the frenzied attacks of the first part of the course. This is a long, slow process of cautious navigation, creeping the submarine slowly towards the mine-lay area. Simon knows there could be all kinds of threats in the vicinity: frigates, or tenders representing patrol craft, or helicopters. He must at all costs remain undetected. The periscope goes up briefly to take navigational fixes, and for a quick visual check on what's around – and then down again. Most of the information about other ships in the area comes from sonar reports. Dai Evans no longer matches the students' actions on the periscope. In fact, he doesn't raise the search periscope at all – it would only serve to increase the danger of detection. But the real point is that he no longer *needs* to watch and check every move the student makes. Teacher can now trust his pupils to be safe.

Nevertheless, Evans checks closely how much time Simon keeps his periscope up. Later he calculates the percentage of time during the exercise that it was raised. He watches Bebbington like a hawk throughout the mine-lay. 'A Chief of Staff once said that this is the stage at which the students become transparent. You see what they're like as people and what you don't see you can feel. I don't believe a leopard can't change his spots; if you're aware of your shortcomings you can take positive steps to eradicate them. I mean, there's no point in giving a man a 700-mph aircraft if he can only fly it at 500 mph – because the man with a 600-mph aircraft, who can fly it to its limit, will have the whip hand. So I've deliberately been putting them under a lot of pressure for the past three weeks.' Dai is concerned that Simon Bebbington has become almost too confident. 'I'm putting him under more pressure at the moment – there's a certain amount of animosity between us. But it's got to be done – it's *got* to be done – they've got to be stretched.'

Bebbington inches his way towards the first mine-lay area. The submarine is barely moving, travelling at less than walking pace. The planesman strives to keep it precisely on depth; the weather is rough on the surface, and if he allows the submarine to come a little too shallow, it is possible that the top of the fin will break the surface at the trough of a wave. The hoist operator watches Simon carefully, waiting for the signal to raise the periscope. Simon himself switches his attention from the navigation chart to the depth gauge, simultaneously listening to sonar reports. There is a patrol craft in the area, part of the enemy forces, and it is approaching. Using mainly sonar, but with the occasional quick periscope look at the enemy and to fix his position on two nearby lighthouses, Simon creeps on. The patrol craft comes closer and closer – first, he's 1000 yards away, eventually he gets as close as 200 yards. A few minutes later, Simon gives the order to fire the mines from the torpedo tubes. A slug of water is released instead, and we turn away. Only half the area is sown, but it takes time to reload with more mines, so we will temporarily move away to a safer distance.

Immediately Evans questions Bebbington: 'Would you have changed anything under different conditions?'

'Yes sir – if it had been calmer on the surface, I wouldn't have released the mines.'

Evans is satisfied. Simon is obviously aware that the air-bubbles associated with the release of mines would have given his position away to the watchful patrol craft if the surface had been calmer. However, Simon judges it is too risky to return later, as planned, and complete the mine-laying. Anyway time is running out: part of David Charlton's next exercise is photographic and it is already well into the afternoon – the light will fade in a few hours.

Simon has another concern which affects his decision not to complete the mine-lay. Every hour, on the hour, a rating lifts a hatch in the main passageway, just outside the galley, and slides his body down into the battery space below the floor. 'The battery' is in fact a series of linked cells that stretch half the length of the submarine, but its current state of charge can be tested from one place. He dips a tube into the electrolyte, measures the reading, and squeezes back up through the hatch. He reports to the duty captain that the battery is now at twenty-six per cent of full charge. This is about as low as it's usually allowed to get.

'Over the past two weeks, we've been able to keep the battery fairly healthy by generating every night,' Simon explains. 'But last night we were only able to charge for a very short period because we were in contact with enemy forces. So the battery is fairly low at the moment – it's adequate for the day's work, if nothing else happens. If we need to evade at speed we simply won't be able to, so it's restricting. We'll have to wait until tonight before we can raise the snort mast to generate again.'

Simon hands over to David Charlton. He has been charged with mine-laying a bay off Arran and photographing another bay just to the north – in fact it's Brodick Bay, where the students stayed in the far-off, luxurious days when they didn't have to sleep on board. To carry out a photographic reconnaissance through the periscope, the student captain must get as close to the shoreline as the depth of water allows. In places he will be within 300 yards of the water's edge. He must plot a precise course along the shoreline, and take photographs at predetermined intervals to provide a panoramic view of the bay. If possible, he will do a double sweep of the periscope whilst photographing, which will create stereoscopic or 3D pictures. Needless to say, the Navy is coy about what coastlines they actually photograph, but the implication is obvious. What is probable is that more than one Royal Navy submarine photographed part of the coast of Argentina during the Falklands conflict, and that to do so effectively it had to go very close. Photography could also be the purpose of the continuous stream of Soviet submarines detected – or not, as the case may be – off the coast of Norway and Sweden.

Charlton is meant to do the photographing first, and then the mine-lay. However, he is concerned about his lack of battery power and feels that if he delays the mine-lay until after the photography, he will have even less chance to carry out what he has judged to be the more important of the two tasks. He has also noticed a frigate waiting off Brodick Bay. So he plans to mine-lay first, then attack the frigate, and finally complete his photographic reconnaissance. But then the sound room reports sonar transmissions, probably from a helicopter sweeping generally for a contact. Charlton immediately slows the submarine right down, explaining that the helicopter recognises and classifies a contact by measuring its speed through the water. He remains, waiting, for some time until the transmissions cease.

It is now late in the day, and with the gathering gloom of the November afternoon reflected in a pinpoint of light at the base of the periscope, Charlton switches to red-light conditions. The battery is down to eighteen per cent. It will now certainly be too late to photograph Brodick Bay, but Charlton's major concern is to continue undetected down the coast of Arran to his mine-lay point.

Finally, with the battery down to fourteen per cent, we complete the task. If this were truly wartime, HMS *Oracle* would now be in the embarrassing position of having to 'snort' with enemy forces not too far away. However, this is Perisher, and Teacher changes the rules, decreeing that we have safe passage to Campbeltown, where we must arrive by six the following morning. So the submarine relaxes, surfaces, and the diesels rattle into action. HMS *Oracle* ploughs through the water at fourteen knots, simultaneously recharging her flagging batteries. At Campbeltown HMS *Otter* also arrives, to prepare for the next and final exercise.

The other half of the course are a little muted. They have just lost Mike Washer.

And then there were six . . .

Charlton and Bebbington are virtually through. They just have one more hurdle to cross. The final day and night of Perisher mark the most dramatic exercise of the past three weeks.

Submarines have always been used to land small groups of troops off enemy coastlines, and the practice continues. They are ideal for the purpose: the submarine can approach the coast quietly at periscope depth, discharge its passengers, then slip away until they are ready to return. But of course there is more to it than that; it is potentially a most hazardous operation because it involves surfacing, so temporarily surrendering the submarine's most precious asset.

The Navy uses the SBS for these operations, the marine equivalent of the SAS. So four strapping young men duly arrive early in the morning, bringing their canoes with them. This being an exercise, they are in fact SBS reserve; one of them is a fireman from Liverpool. The fore-ends crew of HMS *Oracle* spend the morning clearing the area of impedimenta such as camp beds, sleeping bags – and the Captain's windsurfer. George Webster enjoys a sail round the chilly waters of Campbeltown bay before his board is restowed away.

The SBS on each submarine will leave on two two-man canoes. The operation is one that needs rehearsing; it depends on accurate timing and slick teamwork. So the afternoon is spent practising until everyone is satisfied. It has been arranged that David Charlton will command the submarine for the drop, and Simon Bebbington for the pick-up.

By mid-evening the submarine is approaching the coastline that has been selected for the operation. When he is about three miles from the shore, Charlton orders the SBS to take up their positions in the fore-ends. He takes one final all-round look on the periscope, and orders the submarine to surface. As the high-pressure air valves hiss and squeal in the control room, the fore-ends crew start to undo the torpedo-loading hatch. This is a circular hatch just big enough to load a torpedo – or unload a small canoe. *Oracle*'s forecasing breaks the surface – Charlton sees it appear through the periscope and orders the hatch to be opened. In a swarm of hands, feet and equipment, the SBS and their two canoes are manhandled through the hatch and on to the casing. They rest the canoes on the deck and sit in them while the hatch is closed again. As soon as the report 'Torpedo-loading hatch shut and clipped' comes through, Charlton gives the order to dive. As the submarine sinks beneath the surface, the two canoes simply float off.

However, we are still a long way from the shore. The two canoes are tied together by a length of rope. They now manoeuvre themselves into a spaced-out formation, facing the shore. This next part went wrong in the rehearsal, so everyone in the control room holds their breath. Then two distinct rattling sounds come over the sonar loudspeaker. 'Bongle heard bearing 295° . . . Dongle heard bearing 085°.' Each canoe has a crude rattle-device, which one man holds in the water and shakes; the noises are heard quite distinctly by sonar, who can identify each one as either a 'bongle' or 'dongle' and can gauge their relative positions to the submarine.

Soon Charlton can see them through the periscope, and now he confirms that they are in the correct position, straddled a few yards either side of the near-stationary submarine. Carefully he inches the submarine forward until he can see that the periscope has snagged the line that connects the two canoes. He continues moving forward slowly until the canoes are strung out astern of the submarine, with the line taut. Now he can slightly increase speed and tow the four SBS towards their destination. Charlton reminds the hoist operator not to lower the periscope under any circumstances.

This elegant solution brings the canoes and submarine to within one mile of the shore, whereupon Charlton allows the periscope to be lowered, turns the submarine sharply around and heads for a safe distance from the coast, leaving the two canoes to paddle the rest of the way ashore.

An hour later, and Simon Bebbington is anxiously waiting for dongles and bongles. They come, and he starts to manoeuvre the submarine between them. But the night has become even darker since Charlton towed them in, and Simon cannot see the canoes through the periscope at all. He has to guide the submarine purely on sonar information – which should be sufficient, but cannot provide 100 per cent proof that he has snagged the canoes. He strains to see them through his eyepiece, but just cannot. Teacher – who throughout this exercise has deliberately kept in the background – raises the search periscope and invites Simon to check through its superior optics. Still he can see nothing. Teacher checks for himself and invites Simon to look again. Still he can see nothing – neither can David Charlton. 'Make sure you're looking dead astern – they're there,' says Evans with a smile. The two chastened students look again – and can now just pick out the canoes.

Fifteen minutes later the submarine surfaces, picks up the two canoes and their four damp occupants and has dived again in less than ten minutes. The exercise is over. Both students have performed well; in fact they have behaved like submarine captains. Evans clears the wardroom of people and belongings, orders a bottle of champagne from Chirpy Finch, and sends for David Charlton.

'Congratulations, Captain. You've done bloody well – you've gone from strength to strength throughout the course. You've got a lovely style and a good future.'

David Charlton sits, bemused, mumbling his thanks. Evans continues: 'You'll do the staff course from January to August – and then you'll go to command HMS *Opossum*.' Charlton's delight is obvious. Not only has he passed, but he's got the plum job that all the successful students want – command of his own diesel-electric submarine. The only alternative for the successful Perisher, First Lieutenant on a nuclear submarine, is regarded by the students as second-best. They do not relish being demoted to a secondary position after reaching the height of command on Perisher.

Simon is next. Evans shakes his hand too, tells him he's passed, and that he'll be doing two training courses. 'And then you'll go to be First Lieutenant of HMS *Sovereign*.' Simon's face falls a mile, but he cannot suppress a smile. After all, he has passed.

The three men sit down together in the tiny wardroom and celebrate with the bottle of champagne. Just two students out of the five that set out four months ago. For a while none of them quite knows what to say to each other. Suddenly the rules and circumstances of the past four months that have governed their thinking and relationships have changed. Simon and David no longer have to worry about the next briefing, the next exercise, the next debrief with Teacher; they no longer have to worry about passing Perisher. The passing of that concern leaves a vacuum in their exhausted minds. Teacher no longer has to watch, teach, cajole, reprimand, praise or criticise his students; he's made his decision, committed the lives of seventy men into their hands, fulfilled his role. For the first time on the course they should all be able to relax completely – but such adjustments do not come easily. Evans will always be Teacher in his students' eyes. Any submariner who has had command continues to remember his Teacher with respect, and will go to him to try and work out a problem in years to come. The strict adherence to rank and seniority within the service itself puts an invisible barrier between the two Lieutenants and the Commander.

It seems that the happiest man of the three is Dai Evans himself; his smile is so wide that his tired, grey face looks completely round. He is clearly delighted that he has helped to create two new commanding officers.

The two submarines race back to Faslane overnight, arriving early in the morning, and the final ritual of Perisher unfolds. In the guest room of the Clyde Submarine Base's wardroom a huge square table is laid for the traditional Perisher breakfast. The six successful students and their two Teachers sit down to porridge, fried egg, fried croute, fillet steak, grilled kidney, grilled bacon, grilled sausage, grilled tomato, grilled mushrooms, baked beans, toast, marmalade, tea, coffee – followed, at nine o'clock in the morning, by port.

David Charlton was the only Royal Navy Perisher to gain command of a submarine. Nigel Hibbert, from Bob Stevens' group, went on to be First Lieutenant of HMS *Swiftsure*, a nuclear-powered hunter-killer submarine, but both he and Simon Bebbington will eventually take command; and of course David Charlton will eventually have to relinquish command for a spell as First Lieutenant on a nuclear boat before he takes command again. The three successful foreign students all took command of diesel-electric submarines within a few months. Mike Washer went the same route as Tiny Lister, to train to become Principal Warfare Officer on a frigate. After some months of working within the Submarine Service, Gavin McClaren finally succumbed to the failed Perisher tradition and left to join General Service.

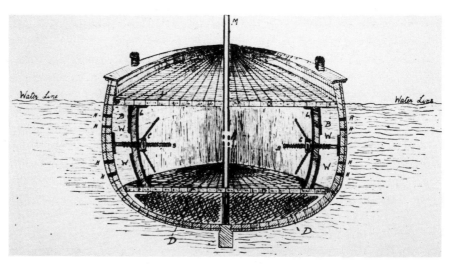

William Bourne's design of 1578 had some advanced features; the screwed leather presses, left and right, and the hollow mast (M) were forerunners of the double hull and the schnorkel.

CHAPTER 3
Submersible to Submarine

The modern nuclear submarine is the perfected version of a concept which started long ago. In 332 BC Alexander the Great is reported to have descended to the depths of the Bosphorus in some kind of diving vessel, made of an iron frame with asses' skins as waterproofing (see page 5). The story is probably apocryphal, but what is significant is that the event was meant to have occurred during the siege of Tyre, and involves one of history's great soldiers. Thus the first mention of underwater activity has military overtones. Boats, aeroplanes and wheeled land transport all started as peaceful devices; the submarine's development is intricately linked with war.

Leonardo da Vinci invented a submarine, of course, but the device he describes in his notebooks was actually intended for peaceful underwater exploration; it was never built. The first design for a truly submersible vessel was by an Englishman. William Bourne lived in the century that saw the first great flowering of Britain's navy; he died in 1588, the year Sir Francis Drake defeated the Spanish Armada. Bourne was a carpenter, gunmaker and writer who in 1578 published *Inventions and Devices* (subtitled 'Very necessary for Generalles, Captaines or leaders of men'). In it he showed that he had grasped the concept of how to submerge a craft and then surface it again. He described a vessel with a rigid wooden outer hull, inside which was a flexible inner hull made of leather. A system of screwed presses allowed this inner hull to be expanded or contracted. Holes in the outer hull let water in, and the craft was submerged by unscrewing the presses, which increased the water-filled space between the two hulls. By reversing the process this extra weight could be 'pumped out', and the vessel floated to the surface. In many ways Bourne's theory matches modern submarine design, which is of course based on the double hull. Compressed air has replaced movable leather skins, but the principle is the same. The only major flaw in Bourne's work is that his design has its strength in the outer hull, whereas it is a submarine's inner hull which takes the strain. Perhaps it was just as well that

Bourne's design was never built; if he had been tempted to any significant depth, the inner leather hull would have buckled and collapsed.

Shortly after Bourne died, a Dutch physician, Cornelius van Drebbel, moved to London as tutor to James I's children. A scientist of vision, his interests included perpetual motion, magic lanterns, explosives – and submersibles. In 1620 he demonstrated a wooden-hulled submersible craft in the Thames, watched by a huge crowd, including the King. The submersible must have been a fair size, because it accommodated a crew of no less than twelve, each manning an oar. The wooden hull was waterproofed with leather, but there was no double hull arrangement to allow flooding and venting of water. The craft was difficult to submerge, but it did drift along with the tide, just below the surface, for long enough to credit van Drebbel with being the first man to travel underwater.

In 1653 a Frenchman, De Son, published grandiose plans for his submersible boat that would 'destroy 100 ships and go from Rotterdam to London and back in one day'. His seventy-three-foot-long vessel was again not a true submarine, having no proper device to allow water to be let in or pumped out, but it did have a sharp, pointed iron ram at either end. De Son may have appreciated the military value of the submersible, but his craft had one major problem: propulsion. He had opted for a clockwork motor driving a paddle-wheel. Unfortunately, when testing the system on land he had forgotten to allow for the pressure of water on the paddle-wheel; when the craft was put in the water the clockwork motor proved quite incapable of turning the wheel.

One hundred and twenty years later, submarines claimed the first of many victims. An English carpenter named Day converted a

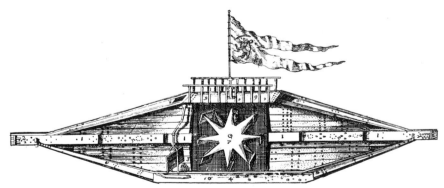

De Son's design of 1653. Despite the inventor's claims that it would 'run as swift as a bird can fly' and 'destroy 100 ships and go from Rotterdam to London in a single day', De Son's clockwork motor failed to move the craft.

Norfolk fishing boat into a watertight submersible, hanging bags of stones from the bottom to provide ballast and, when released, buoyancy. After a successful experimental 'dive' to about thirty feet in the Norfolk Broads, Day financed his next design by suggesting to a gambler, a certain Mr Blake, that he should bet his colleagues that Day could not submerge to 100 feet for twelve hours (Day was to take ten per cent of Blake's winnings). Day built his boat, a sloop of fifty tons, and took it to Plymouth Sound for the gamblers to see. On 20 June 1774 he climbed in, fastened the hatch tightly shut, and sank to the bottom of the sea – a depth of some 130 feet. It was the last that anyone saw of the bold carpenter. The sloop has never been found, but must have been crushed to smithereens by the tremendous pressure of water.

So far, despite some brave and ingenious attempts, no one had come near a practical submersible craft which would dive and surface, move underwater and keep its occupants alive. It took a war to provide such a device – the American War of Independence.

The British fleet's blockade of the Eastern-seaboard ports was proving extremely burdensome to the Colonists. Roads were few and inadequate, and supplies which would normally be moved by sea were stuck fast in harbours. The Colonists had virtually no Navy of their own, and desperately needed a secret weapon with which to surprise the English. David Bushnell, an elderly undergraduate at Yale College, had been experimenting with exploding gunpowder underwater. He realised that such a device, in the form of a mine, could be fatal if attached to the underside of the blockading ships. Bushnell's other great interest had always been underwater craft, and so he set about designing a method of delivering these primitive mines. What emerged was the *Turtle*, the world's first properly

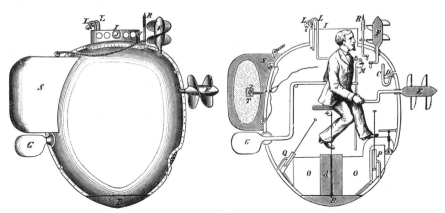

Bushnell's *Turtle* and its frantically busy operator.

armed submarine. It did not bear much resemblance to its twentieth-century successors – its name stemmed from its similarity to two turtle's eggs fixed together. Although ugly and in some ways impractical, the *Turtle* embodied many original and useful ideas. Its resemblance to a barrel, for instance, meant it probably had some of that vessel's inherent strength. It was not double-hulled, but did boast an internal water tank, which could be flooded to allow the craft to sink and pumped out by foot to provide buoyancy again. To keep the odd-shaped vessel upright it had a lead ballast-keel, part of which could be jettisoned in an emergency. A watertight hatch at the top contained three small windows through which the operator could see where he was going. Forward motion was provided by one hand-operated propeller, and vertical movement by another similar device on top of the craft. The tiller for the small rudder seems to have been tucked under the busy operator's left arm. *Turtle*'s armament was ingenious. On the outside was an auger, one end of which was attached by a short line to a 150-lb charge of gunpowder. The idea was to drill into the hull of one of the blockading ships, release both the auger and its attached charge, and get as far away as possible before the clockwork delay-mechanism exploded the charge.

On the night of 6 September 1776, two rowing boats towed the *Turtle*, manned by the intrepid Sergeant Ezra Lee, from the Battery on Manhattan Island to within a few hundred yards of the frigate HMS *Eagle*, the flagship of the British fleet blockading New York. The sea was absolutely calm, so Lee could keep the top hatch open as the tide drifted the *Turtle* towards the fleet. Unfortunately he was swept right past the ships, the *Turtle*'s own propulsion proving incapable of counteracting the strong current. But Lee waited patiently until the tide turned, whereupon he was swept back towards the fleet again. Now he could shut the hatch, flood the water tank to trim down, and creep towards the *Eagle*. Lee knew he had about half an hour before the air in the *Turtle* became poisonous, so he quickly manoeuvred the craft underneath the frigate and started to drill – only to discover that its copper sheathing was too hard for his auger to penetrate. After two attempts at different points in the hull, Lee started to become drowsy and had to abandon the attack. He surfaced and started drifting back towards Manhattan. But by now dawn was breaking and some soldiers on Governors' Island spotted him and gave chase in rowing boats. Lee jettisoned his 150 lbs of gunpowder, which promptly exploded in his startled pursuers' faces, and he escaped safely. *Turtle* had failed in its primary objective – but only just. Given a sharper auger, the *Eagle* could well have been sunk; in which case the rest of the fleet would have had to withdraw some considerable distance, and the effectiveness of the blockade might have been significantly reduced. It was very nearly the first example of submarine deterrence.

It is possible – although there is no evidence to support the notion – that the notoriety achieved by the *Turtle* story, allied with the privations of the War of Independence, were significant factors in the psychological development of an 11-year-old boy living in Little Britain, Pennsylvania. Robert Fulton grew up to be an idealist who was dedicated to the abolition of war and the promotion of free trade. He became an artist, engineer and inventor determined to put his considerable talents to use by inventing a device which would help to make war redundant. He reasoned that a truly effective submarine would be such a threat to the great navies of the world that those countries who enjoyed military and commercial dominance through the strength of their sea power would no longer, faced with the underwater threat, be able to rely on their fleets. No one country, therefore, would ever achieve world dominance again – and so the submarine would ensure universal peace and free trade. It is an interesting theory, and seems to pick up the emerging theme of the submarine as a deterrent. However, Fulton's efforts were to have a quite different effect on the world's attitudes towards submarines.

Fulton's idealism naturally attracted him to late eighteenth-century France, which was then under blockade by the powerful English fleet. In 1797 he wrote to the French Directory outlining his plan for the building of the submarine *Nautilus*. Fulton suggested a remarkably mercenary deal for one so idealistic: that he should receive 4000 francs for the destruction of every British ship of forty guns or more, and 2000 francs for every one of less than forty guns. Fulton was convinced that submarines would be regarded in the same light as fireships, which were so despised as a dishonourable method of war that their crews, if captured, were summarily executed. (This is the first discernible hint that submarine warfare was somehow unfair and underhand, and less acceptable than the cannon-balls and grapeshot of surface warfare.) He suggested to the French that if anyone operating a submarine were captured and mistreated, the government should undertake reprisals on British prisoners, matching the mistreatment but quadrupling the numbers.

A month later the Minister of Marine replied, accepting most of Fulton's terms but wisely refusing any guarantee of retaliation against British prisoners of war, since there were only one third as many as French prisoners in British hands. The Minister also expressed his distaste at this underhand method of destroying enemy warships. Undeterred, Fulton persisted. He succeeded in having his proposals examined by a Naval Commission, which wrote a favourable report, but he still did not persuade the Directory to grant him funds. Finally, when the Directory was overthrown, his luck turned. The new Minister had been on the Commission which had praised his design, and Fulton received 10,000 francs for an experimental submarine.

Nautilus was an interesting craft: twenty-one feet long, built of copper sheeting over iron frames, it could withstand water pressure at twenty-five feet. It had a sail which could be raised on a hinged mast for surface running and a muscle-operated propeller for underwater use. Internal water tanks could be flooded or vented for diving and surfacing, and this submarine had one feature which many later versions were to include – the depth-keeping rear hydroplane. It was an eminently practical craft and its trials went well, with dives of up to one hour. However, its armament was less effective; perhaps the result of its idealistic inventor being unable or unwilling to engineer an efficient tool of destruction. It was a complicated system of detachable explosives, a little like that used by the *Turtle*, and not much more effective.

The successful trials encouraged Fulton to ask for more money to build a bigger and better version. This was not forthcoming and all he got was a small sum to refit *Nautilus* and use it in anger against the British fleet. He continued with the trials and improved his submarine, although he did not carry out any attacks. By July 1801, the copper and iron craft was corroding badly and starting to leak. Fulton was anxious to build a new one, but his ally had now left the Ministry of Marine, and his replacement, Admiral de Crès, took a very different view. 'Your invention is good only for Algerians and pirates,' he thundered disdainfully.

By now rumours of this French secret weapon had caused the British to send agents to tempt Fulton to England – where he finally went, disillusioned, in 1804. By now Fulton had improved *Nautilus*'s armament into a primitive torpedo. Pitt was interested in his ideas and appointed a commission to investigate them. Its conclusions were significant. It condemned submersibles as impractical, but did acknowledge the value of the torpedo. Fulton carried out a successful demonstration of one of these on a 200-ton Danish brig, after which a shocked but grimly realistic Admiral the Earl St Vincent growled: 'Pitt was the greatest fool that ever existed to encourage a mode of warfare which those who commanded the seas did not want, and which, if successful, would deprive them of it.' The sentiment both confirms Fulton's original reasons for building a submarine and sets the tone for the Royal Navy's attitude towards them for well over 100 years.

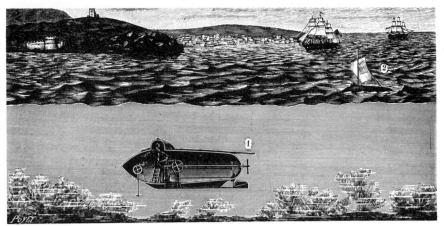

Fulton's *Nautilus* (1) submerged, (2) with sail hoisted, did not become a particularly successful submersible design.

Fulton and his plans received other, less complimentary reviews. The *Naval Chronicle* called his ideas 'revolting to every principle', slanderously referred to him as a 'crafty, murderous ruffian' and, working themselves into a lather of indignation, called his submarines 'such detestable machines, that promise destruction to maritime establishments'. Interest in his plans waned. He was paid for his work and returned to his native America, where his interest switched to steam propulsion systems for surface ships. But his premise, unwittingly underlined by the Earl St Vincent, that submarines would be of more value to the weaker naval powers, was to be fully justified in the American Civil War.

The Confederates suffered grievously from the effects of a sea blockade by the Union forces. The Northerners not only had many more warships, but they also boasted the first of the 'ironclads', which were virtually immune from conventional cannon-fire. The Southerners determined to break the blockade with submersibles – the first time that a government, rather than an individual inventor, had taken the initiative in this type of warfare.

The boats that resulted were innovatory in two ways. Firstly, they were the first, other than De Son's clockwork disaster, to use mechanical rather than human propulsion. Each contained a small steam engine which propelled them at about five knots. Secondly, they carried armament which, unlike their predecessors', was potentially effective. An underwater bomb was fixed to a long wooden spar facing forward on the outside of the submarine – not unlike the lance of a medieval knight. The boats themselves were built of iron, and were not submarines in the true sense but submersibles. With the funnels their steam engines required, they could only trim down so that their bulk was running just below the surface, with part of their deck, including an open hatch, and the tall funnel still above the surface. The intention was that the enemy ships would not see them until it was too late to depress their guns sufficiently to hit them. These little boats, it was hoped, would prove giant killers; thus they were called 'Davids'. Their great weakness was the open hatch, which could so easily lead to swamping.

On 5 October 1863, a 'David' set out from Charleston, South Carolina, and headed for the federal battleship *Ironsides*. With the hatch just above the surface, it came to within a few yards of the ironclad's side, and detonated its spar torpedo. A huge explosion followed and *Ironsides'* engine room began to fill with water, but when the panic subsided, the 'David' was nowhere to be seen. It had been swamped by the blast of the explosion – and *Ironsides* survived.

The Confederates now modified their submersible to make it a true submarine. A Captain Horace Hunley of the Confederate Army produced a design which reverted to hand propulsion, with no less than eight men manning a rotating crankshaft in a long, slim hull. The *H. L. Hunley* was a sizeable craft, sixty feet long, and the effort required to propel her consumed nearly as much oxygen as the steam engines in the 'Davids'. *H. L. Hunley* had to surface frequently to allow fresh air through the hatch, thus making the submarine as vulnerable to swamping as its predecessor. This boat seems to have had a disastrous short life. During trials she had accident after accident, sinking several times, and killing about thirty of her volunteer crew, including her inventor. Despite these setbacks, and despite the great difficulties experienced in controlling her when dived, on the night of 17 October 1864 she was sent into action. The target was the wooden corvette *Housatonic*, thirteen guns, anchored off Charleston. There were already intelligence rumours of secret Confederate weapons floating around the Northerners' fleet. The *H. L. Hunley* was as usual proving difficult to control when trimmed right down, and was probably 'banana-ing' – a modern submarine term for a roller-coaster course caused by poor trim and handling – as she approached the *Housatonic*. She was spotted on one of her inadvertent visits to the surface, and the corvette's guns were run out and aimed – but the *Hunley* was now too close and the guns could not be sufficiently depressed. The clumsy submersible lumbered right up to the helpless warship and detonated its single spar torpedo. The *Housatonic* rocked with the explosion, and almost immediately began to sink. She soon settled on the shallow bottom, the first victim

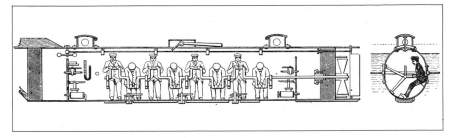

The *H. L. Hunley*, which in 1863 became the first submersible to sink a warship. The Confederate craft was swamped by its own torpedo's explosion and sank with all hands.

An early Confederate steam-powered 'David' submersible aground in Charleston Harbour, South Carolina, 1865.

of submarine warfare. But there was no sign of the *H. L. Hunley*. The Confederate submarine had somehow been destroyed by its own explosion and, true to form, had sunk to the bottom, taking her brave crew of nine with her.

Over the next thirty years there were various efforts around the world to construct the definitive submarine. The French went in for sheer size with their 410-ton *Le Plongeur*, but that proved uncontrollable underwater. The Russians tried a pedal-powered submarine. The English stayed in the race in the form of the Reverend George William Garrett, a curate in Liverpool. His aim,

Submarine pioneers took many unexpected forms; the Reverend George William Garrett with his 'Resurgam' in 1879.

not surprisingly, was to produce a submarine for peaceful purposes of exploration. He fitted it with a steam engine whose oversize boiler was to provide a head of steam after the furnace had been shut down for diving. He called his craft 'Resurgam', but regrettably it sank with all three hands on its maiden voyage.

By the very end of the nineteenth century, it was clear that there were certain new technologies that should allow submarine development to take a great leap forward. The internal-combustion engine, the electric motor, the storage of electricity, the development of the torpedo, and improved shipbuilding techniques all needed to be brought together into one truly workable design. With Britain still remaining aloof, the two most interested countries were France and America. In the 1890s, both countries ran competitions to encourage their various inventors.

In France, M. Laubeuf, an ex-Engineer-in-Chief of the Navy, won a gold medal for his design for a submarine called the *Narval*. This was a dual-purpose vessel, whose hull design made her most suitable for surface running, where she would spend most of her time; submerging was only to be done when necessary for an attack. This philosophy, of the 'submersible' rather than the true submarine, continued in submarine design right up to the advent of the nuclear-powered submarine in the 1950s. Only then did the shape change from one principally suited to surface-running to a sleek, whale- or dolphin-like outline whose natural habitat was underwater.

The *Narval* contained two vital features: the double hull and the method of propulsion. Not since Bourne's design of 1578, with its expanding leather inner skin, had anyone used the idea of achieving positive, negative and neutral buoyancy through the flooding and

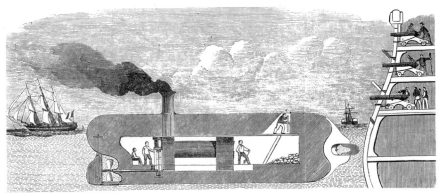

One of the weirder submersible designs of the nineteenth century.
Fortunately this 'anti-invasion floating mortar' with its 'monster
self-exploding shell' was never built.

venting of large tanks outside the main pressure hull of the
submarine. For propulsion the *Narval* had a steam engine for
surface-running (fired by oil, itself an advanced concept in 1898) and
electric motors for submerged running. M. Laubeuf incorporated the
simple but effective notion of using the steam engine to recharge the
electric motors' batteries whilst on the surface, thus greatly increasing
the submarine's underwater capability. Shutting down the steam
engine before diving was a lengthy business, as was refiring it after
surfacing, but nevertheless this submarine, with its four torpedo
launchers, convinced the French Navy that this type of craft was
certainly useful for coastal operations, and possibly further afield too.
There was great public enthusiasm for submarines in France, not least
because they were seen as a new weapon in the continuing tension
with England. A public appeal organised by *Le Matin* raised sufficient
funds for two submarines, and the government ordered eight more.
Across the Channel, however, the Royal Navy still disdained any
involvement with the concept. Fortunately for them, the competition
in America was to bring them an unforeseen benefit.

John P. Holland, a schoolmaster from County Clare, had been
obsessively working on submarine development ever since he
emigrated to America in 1873. Having experienced the great Irish
potato famine of 1840, he was not fond of the British and was
determined that his submarines should one day be used against them.
In this he was helped by the Fenian Society, who partially funded his
early designs. In 1884 they even purloined one of his prototypes,
hoping to use it against the British; but without its inventor, the boat
proved too difficult to control. Holland tried in vain to interest the US

Left J. P. Holland, the schoolmaster from County Clare who emigrated to America and became the father of modern submarines.

Below Simon Lake's 'Argonaut', complete with wheels, in Baltimore. Behind it is Holland's 'Plunger'.

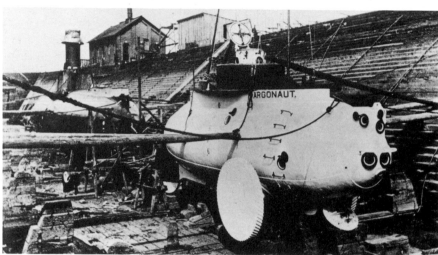

Navy. Instead, he had to coax a variety of businessmen into funding his designs which, although progressing, suffered endless setbacks. When the US Navy finally initiated a competition in 1895, the rules were absurdly strict, demanding designs with much greater speed and endurance than anything previously conceived. But Holland produced a design which, in theory at least, could satisfy the requirements. Called the 'Plunger', it won the competition. This is perhaps not too surprising, since his principal competitor was a certain Simon Lake, who was convinced that the answer to the problem of submarines' propulsion was wheels. Lake's 'Argonaut' was meant to trundle along at the bottom of the ocean, using a searchlight to find its way – and, presumably, to avoid any rocks and obstacles.

'Plunger' may have won the competition, but Holland knew that the compromises he had made to satisfy the rules meant that it could never work properly. So, although the 'Plunger' was already under construction, he borrowed $25,000 from a generous New York benefactress and designed yet another submarine – his eighth in twenty years. The 'Holland' was smaller than the 'Plunger', and in theory inferior because it was much less powerful; but it was practical. A small petrol engine for surface-running replaced the elaborate steam engines of its predecessors, and also charged the batteries for the electric motor. A single reloadable torpedo tube provided its armament. Interestingly, the shape of the hull was closer to the tear-drop of the modern nuclear submarine than any other design in the intervening half-century.

Holland's years of experience paid off. The submarine worked well, and impressed the authorities much more than the still only half-finished 'Plunger'. After her final official trial in 1899 one of the US naval officers wrote: 'I report my belief that the "Holland" is a successful and veritable submarine torpedo boat, capable of making an attack on an enemy unseen and undetectable, and that, therefore, she is an Engine of Warfare of terrible potency which the Government must necessarily adopt in its Service.'

The US Navy bought the 'Holland' for $165,000, ordered another, bigger, prototype, and subsequently, in June 1900, five more boats based on the new design. But J. P. Holland did not benefit greatly from this success. His earlier lack of funds had forced him to sell all his patents to his backers, the Electric Boat Co. Holland became their chief engineer, but never had a seat on the board; it seems a cruel fate for such a successful pioneer.

J. P. Holland was the last of a long and noble line of individual submarine inventors. From William Bourne onwards, the pioneers of

Lake's 'Protector' was a successor to his 'Argonaut'. He still favoured wheels, albeit retractable. Lake must have been a talented salesman; he sold five to the US Government and four to the Russians.

Europe and America had risked their fortunes and their lives pursuing a dream that was theoretically feasible but constantly frustrated by technological inadequacy. Now, Holland's submarines in America and the French designs in Europe were becoming highly practical boats. But their success inevitably meant that further development was to be firmly in the hands of companies and governments. As the new century began, there was a positive flowering of submarine development in Europe and America; but we hear less and less of those pioneer inventors, more and more of influential admirals and bankers.

It was fortunate for Great Britain that bankers were taking an interest – because her admirals still were not. In 1899 Lord Rothschild arranged a meeting between Isaac Rice, President of the Electric Boat Co., and the Admiralty. The US Navy was still arguing about how many boats it should order, so meanwhile Rice was anxious to exploit the Holland design as much as possible. He arrived in a Britain sharply divided over the ethics and efficacy of the submarine. Britain's fleet was still extraordinarily powerful, and many of her admirals simply would not accept the need for submarine boats, which had always been associated with weaker naval powers. Some could see the value of the new type of warfare but preferred to ignore it in the hope that it would go away. Others, such as Admiral of the Fleet Sir Arthur Wilson, reacted more strongly. It was he who remarked that submarines were 'underhand, unfair and damned un-English . . . we cannot stop invention in this direction, but we can avoid doing anything to encourage it'.

Not all of Britain's Naval Establishment were quite so blinkered. Rice nearly succeeded in securing an order to build a Holland submarine in the US, for shipment to Britain, for the princely sum of £34,000. But the Admiralty, realising the political unacceptability of Britain's Navy taking delivery of even a prototype from a foreign shipyard, changed the arrangement, and the Vickers company built the boat under licence from the Electric Boat Co. – the first of a long line of submarines to be built in Barrow-in-Furness. 'Holland I' was launched in 1902. Innovative though it was, Holland's design had many faults – not least the low freeboard and open hatch, which, like the 'David', made it vulnerable to swamping. So within months Vickers produced a modified design, bigger, more powerful, and with a much higher fin providing an insurance against swamping.

It is surely significant that, while the French, currently in the forefront of submarine development, were calling their boats such fine and impressive names as *Gustav Zédé* and *Sirène*, the first

Left Admiral of the Fleet Sir Arthur Wilson.

Below Ancient and modern. The Royal Navy's submarine 'No. 3' passing Nelson's flagship *Victory* in Portsmouth Harbour in 1904.

Bottom The 'A' class was a direct development of the Holland. It featured a much higher fin, to avoid the danger of swamping.

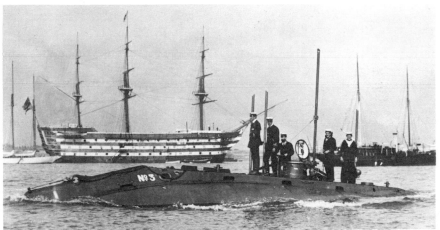

British-designed submarine was not dignified with a name at all, just a designation: A1. More followed, and Britain's first submarine squadron was born. But they were all used essentially for coastal, defensive work. It was the French who were developing the submarine into a longer-range, offensive weapon. By June 1901 they had no fewer than fourteen in operation and a further twenty-five under construction. In trials, their submarines proved capable of hitting battleships from a considerable distance. But in 1902 a change of government brought a change in attitude, and France's building programme was dramatically pruned.

The consequences were considerable. A young Spanish engineer, R. d'Equevilley, offered plans for a new submarine to the French Ministry of Marine. Disillusioned by their refusal, he took them across the border to Germany, where the giant armament corporation of Krupp decided to build a small working model of seventeen tons.

Germany had no apparent need of submarines; its coastline was short, the water shallow, and anyway German admirals were big-ship men, much like Britain's. Although d'Equevilley's model led to a larger design, 116 feet long and capable of nine knots when submerged, the first purchasers were the Russian Navy, who bought three. But in 1906 the German Government ordered Unterseeboot Eins, or U1.

Between the turn of the century and 1914, submarines developed at a remarkable pace. By the time the First World War broke out, they were efficient fighting machines, whose basic design was to remain substantially unaltered until the advent of the nuclear submarine of the 1950s. They were not, however, without problems.

In Britain, the A class was followed by the B and C classes, all developed from Holland's original design. Although basically sound, these boats had many faults. Their petrol engines released dangerous fumes and were always in danger of exploding, and the batteries that powered their electric motors tended to give off hydrogen and corrode very quickly. When dived, they were difficult to control, porpoising up and down from deep to surface. It goes without saying that conditions inside were primitive. There was little room for such niceties as toilets or washing facilities, and after a three-day voyage – about the maximum endurance for these early craft – the state of the interior does not bear thinking about.

The D class, the first of which was delivered in 1909, was a great improvement. It featured external ballast tanks, pioneered on the French *Narval* fifteen years before. These were much safer than the internal tanks of the Holland-based A, B and C classes, which took up valuable interior space, and were potentially dangerous since they contained water at a pressure much higher than that inside the hull. The other major advance was the switch to the newly invented diesel engine. Diesel is a less volatile fuel than petrol, and its fumes, although unpleasant, are nowhere near as dangerous. The Vickers diesels that powered British submarines until after the 1914–18 war were bulky objects, but effective and reliable. They had one uniquely practical feature: if one of the cylinders stopped working, the engineers could 'sling the piston' – disconnect it from the crankshaft – and limp home on the remaining cylinders.

The D class and its successor the E class were the first of Britain's long-range submarines. They had the endurance to venture beyond the coasts and harbours into distant oceans. The problem was that no one quite knew how to use them.

One of Britain's original justifications for ordering the Holland submarines had been that it was vital to discover how these nuisances worked in order to develop defences against them. It was never envisaged that the world's greatest Navy would actually need to use them itself. But their value as local coastal-defensive craft was soon appreciated; it was thinking beyond that which the Naval Establishment found difficult. Admiral Sir John Fisher, who had become First Sea Lord in 1904, was a strong supporter of submarines. In a letter to a fellow Admiral he expostulated: 'It is astounding to me, perfectly astounding, how the very best amongst us fail to realise the vast impending revolution in naval warfare and naval strategy that the submarine will accomplish.' He wanted more submarines – and got them – but seemed always to consider that the revolution would be confined to coastal defence. He did however predict that the submarine could provide a far better and wider protection than shore batteries, extending the defended areas around ports and linking them together, creating a complete defence against the blockade. This is the submarine's first major influence on naval tactics.

The reluctance to see submarines in any offensive role was as much due to Britain's unerring belief in the battleship, of which it possessed more than any other navy, as to the belief that the dirty and uncomfortable world of submarines was really no occupation for fine minds and decent characters. Submarines, ostracised by the rest of the Navy, became a self-contained unit which ignored tactical development in favour of technical advances. But attitudes were slowly changing.

Strangely, it was that most scathing of officers, Admiral Wilson, who earlier had denounced the submarine as so un-English, who was responsible for a basic advance in the Navy's use of submarines. He must have softened a little in his attitude by the time he replaced Fisher as First Sea Lord in 1910. He had been deeply impressed by the

Edwardian Britain possessed more battleships than any other Navy; so resistance to scruffy submarines was hardly surprising.

exploits of the D1 which, earlier in the year, had 'sunk' two cruisers during manoeuvres off Scotland. He realised that the polarisation of submariners' and surface-sailors' positions was absurd and unproductive, and appointed an up-and-coming officer, Captain Roger Keyes, as the new Inspecting Captain of Submarines.

Keyes had recently commanded a cruiser, and so was no submarine specialist, but neither was he a blinkered big-ship man, and he set to work to establish the future of the submarine in the British Navy. One of his first achievements was to abolish the absurd rule that still required an escorting ship with red flags to accompany submarines. Now, when submarines were on manoeuvres, they could perform as genuine warships and exploit their invisibility. Keyes reorganised the submarine fleet's training, questioned their tactics, had more submarines built, and generally licked them into shape. With his contacts in the surface fleet, he was able to spread the word that the submarine was an animal worth taking seriously; this was becoming all too apparent anyway, with more and more manoeuvres involving submarines. Keyes was taking submarines away from ports and harbours, and using them against the Fleet at sea.

The submarine was, of course, much slower than surface ships, so it only had a single chance to fire its torpedo as the Fleet passed. The artificiality of manoeuvres allowed submarines to be in the right place at the right time, awaiting the arrival of the Fleet. In reality it would be extremely difficult for a few slow submarines to find and attack a group of warships at sea. The answer was to build more and more, which Britain was struggling to do.

In 1912 an event of no small significance happened: two experimental submarines, to be built at Vickers' and at Scott's of Greenock, would be given *names*. They were to be called *Swordfish* and *Nautilus* – the latter having the retrograde feature of steam propulsion for greater speed. Coupled with the appointment as First Lord of the Admiralty of Winston Churchill, who took a great interest in submarines, the future was beginning to look a lot better.

At the same time Germany was also increasing production of submarines. These were powerful, well-armed boats, with larger torpedoes and, most important, the long-range capacity to patrol off another country's shore. At this stage, however, the Germans were barely more enlightened than the British about the potential power of the submarine. They did see them as a useful balance to Britain's dominating battleship, but not as much more. It was Britain's Admiral Fisher who put his finger on the real value of submarines to Germany – and in the process frightened and outraged his colleagues at the Admiralty so deeply that they proceeded to suppress his revolutionary ideas.

Fisher made the now-obvious prediction that the submarine could be used in war to sink merchant vessels. Admitting that was an 'inhuman and barbarous' practice, which would 'fill the world with horror', he pointed out that 'this submarine menace is a truly terrible one for Great Britain and British commerce alike'. His paper was suppressed, and those who did see it refused to accept its most revolutionary suggestion. Churchill himself wrote in January 1914, 'I am not convinced . . . of the use of the submarine to sink merchant vessels. I do not believe this could ever be done by a civilised power.' But Fisher's answer was already contained within the paper, in the grim remark, 'The essence of war is violence, and moderation in war is imbecility.'

Doubtless the expressions of naval outrage at Fisher's suggestion were genuine, but it is extraordinary that no one else even considered this use of submarines as a possibility. If they had, it would have highlighted another deficiency in the Admiralty's efforts: despite buying Holland's design twelve years previously, ostensibly to develop anti-submarine methods, no such techniques yet existed. Indeed, in 1912 a certain Lieutenant Layton took his submarine D2 up the Firth of Forth, without being detected by any of the lookouts, and 'torpedoed' his own depot ship. So, by 1914, the submarine had proved itself capable of attacking ships in harbour, defending whole coastlines against blockade, and sinking cruisers and battleships at sea. It had also been recognised by at least one man that it could cut off a maritime nation's life-blood. The stage was set for the first real test of the submarine as an engine of war.

World War I was ultimately to justify every fear that the British Naval Establishment had expressed over the value of submarines to an inferior naval power. The new weapon of war was to bring the world's premier maritime nation to its knees.

On 2 September 1914 the first blow was struck. The German submarine U21, recharging her batteries off the Firth of Forth, could not believe her luck when, over the horizon, appeared the British light cruiser *Pathfinder*. Falling over themselves to scramble into position, the crew of thirty-eight shut off the diesels, hurriedly clipped the hatches and flooded the ballast tanks. But the submarine's major limitation, lack of underwater speed, frustrated their plans. *Pathfinder* sailed unconcernedly away, oblivious to the lurking U21, which surfaced and continued charging. But three hours later their luck returned. *Pathfinder* reappeared, on a perfect course for U21 to attack. Its commander, Lt Cdr Hersing, approached the cruiser carefully. The weather had worsened and the heavy swell kept breaking over the periscope. Depth-keeping was difficult, with the constant danger of the submarine breaking surface and revealing its position. The fore-ends' crew checked the torpedo-firing system for the last time, Hersing took a final range and bearing, and fired the torpedo. *Pathfinder* steamed on, still quite unaware of the threat. The torpedo hissed out of its tube and sped towards its target. Would the built-in depth control work, or would the torpedo pass harmlessly underneath the target? If it did hit, would it explode? Had Hersing got the firing bearing right?

Four minutes later, HMS *Pathfinder* had sunk. The torpedo had hit close to the ship's own magazine and the two explosions ripped her apart. Out of a crew of 296, 259 died. This was the first warship to be sunk by a submarine since the *Housatonic* took the *H. L. Hunley* to the bottom with her. U21 suffered no such fate. Her elated crew turned her safely away from the scene of destruction and sought other prey.

It would be comforting to write that this incident taught the British fleet a lesson, and that in the future a sharper lookout was kept for submarines; but it does not seem to have been so. As dawn was breaking on 12 September, U9, commanded by the intrepid Lt Otto Weddigen, sighted, torpedoed and sank the ageing British cruiser HMS *Aboukir*. She had been steaming slowly and unconcernedly with her two elderly companions, HMS *Hague* and *Cressy*, off the Dutch coast. No attempt had been made to vary speed or course because of the submarine threat; presumably the continuing arrogance of the fleet assumed that there was no threat. Indeed, even

an einem Tag!

„ABOUKIR"

„HOGUE"

„CRESSY"

Kapitänleutnant Weddigen
starb den Heldentod auf U 29

'In one day!' screams the newspaper headline. On 22 September 1914 Otto Weddigen in U9 (*left*) accounted for 36,000 tons of British warships, and 1400 officers and men, in less than one hour.

after *Aboukir* was struck, the *Hague* must have assumed it had been a mine that did the damage, because she went to the aid of the stricken cruiser. U9, recovering from the shock waves of her own torpedo explosion, fired another – and the *Hague* was hit. Again the submarine was rocked by the explosion, and briefly broke surface. The *Hague*, sinking but on an even keel, fired at the wallowing submarine, to no avail. Five minutes later the cruiser sank.

HMS *Cressy*, by now surely fully aware that mines were not responsible for the carnage, nevertheless made no attempt to escape, preferring to go to the rescue of the other ships' crews. But Weddigen had no intention of allowing such sentiment to cloud his judgement and, reloading his torpedo tubes, he closed in. At the last moment his periscope was sighted. The cruiser finally came to her senses and desperately tried to make a run for it, black smoke pouring from her funnels. But it was much too late for such a gesture; she was hit by two torpedoes and soon rolled right over. Three cruisers and 1400 men had been destroyed by one small submarine with a crew of less than forty.

Still the lessons were not fully learned. Less than a month later the same submarine, with the same commander, was off the coast of Aberdeen when several warships came into sight. They were dutifully zigzagging and changing speed, and Weddigen was unable to manoeuvre himself into a firing position; his underwater speed was too limited. But then two of the cruisers, *Hawke* and *Endymion*, actually stopped. Coaxing every available amp from his inadequate batteries, Weddigen started to close on the cruisers, which were calmly transferring mail. Shortly afterwards *Hawke* was hit and sank within minutes.

U9's activity had far-reaching effects. Other German submarines had been sighted around the coast of Scotland, and the safety of the fleet, at anchor in Scapa Flow, was thrown into doubt. In fact there were only two U-boats in the area, but the threat was seen to be great and the fleet was ordered to raise steam. After a night of alarums and excursions, during which a dozen non-existent submarines were sighted, it set sail from Scapa Flow for Lough Swilly in Ireland and Loch-na-Keal in Mull. The fleet arrived unmolested, but it was an ignominious manoeuvre for the world's most powerful Navy. The submarine was becoming a threat merely by its presence.

Yet with proper tactics it should not have been too difficult for any surface warship to evade submarine attack. The destroyers, cruisers and battleships all enjoyed much greater speed than the submerged submarine; the submarines' torpedoes were short-range – less than a mile – and unreliable; and although the older British warships such as

Aboukir were vulnerable, the more modern ships were well armoured and could withstand the limited explosive charge of the early torpedoes. In addition, the U-boats took a long time to dive and if surprised on the surface were sitting targets for gunfire or ramming. Indeed, the successful Otto Weddigen's career lasted only a matter of months: in March 1915 he was rammed and sunk by HMS *Dreadnought*.

By now the endurance of the German boats had been extended far beyond what had been considered possible before the war began. Continuous patrols of anything up to three weeks were becoming commonplace. These allowed the U-boats to avoid the English Channel, now heavily defended, and harass the western coasts of Britain by travelling around the north of Scotland. However, they also meant that the crews had to suffer the privations of submarine life for longer too. American submarines were known as 'pig-boats' during this war; but the description could have applied equally well to the submarines of Britain and Germany. Conditions were appalling. Underwater, the cold Atlantic made the inside of the boat dank and chilly; fresh food soon went bad, and for most of the patrol the crew lived on tins. There was little fresh water, and washing was way down the priority list. Toilet facilities were crude, with just one lavatory per submarine; the stench of stale air, urine, chlorine from the battery, and diesel fuel was sickening. On the surface, some fresh air entered through the open hatches, but there were no fans to encourage proper circulation. Sleep became almost impossible. Even if men eventually became accustomed to the constant rattling of the diesels, there were always noisy repairs to do, with the hammering echoing down the steel hull. Or a heavy torpedo would have to be manhandled from storage in the stern of the submarine right to the fore-ends, with accompanying shouts, curses and disruption. Then, just when the repairs were finished, the torpedo safely in its rack and the diesels a soft drone in fatigue-drugged minds, the klaxon would blare out, signalling a crash dive. However tired, all hands had to leap out of their bunks and stagger to their action stations, ready for the next attack.

British submarines had been active during the first few months of the war, but had not had the spectacular successes of their German counterparts. They were used principally in the Heligoland Bight area, to reinforce the blockade of German ports and help with surface-warship actions against the German Navy. In fact, the German fleet stayed sensibly out of harm's way, but the D- and E-class boats did provide valuable reconnaissance information.

The cramped living quarters of
U-boats (*left*) were matched in
British submarines such as E34
(*below*). A rating prepares a meal
for the lieutenant in his easy chair
and the navigator who, judging by
his oilskins, has just come down
from the bridge.

Any attempt to mount combined operations between surface ships
and submarines was hampered by the latter's slow speed and poor
wireless sets. Communication between British submarines and their
bases was absurdly difficult. Their sets were good for only about forty
miles, and so they had to resort to primitive methods – including
pigeons. The bird would be released from the submarine with
encoded messages for the Admiralty. After flying for anything up to
150 miles, it would arrive at its owner's trap. He would telegraph the

contents to the Admiralty, who would enjoy the decoded message many hours after it had been sent. There is no record of carrier pigeons flying back to submarines, and so communication must have been entirely one way.

The submarine was proving itself most effective as a lone raider. Within a few weeks of the outbreak of war D5 had come close to upstaging U21's success. She discovered the German cruiser *Rostock* in the Heligoland Bight and, despite the screen of destroyers, managed to get within 600 yards of the target. But the two torpedoes she fired passed straight underneath the cruiser. It seems that the dummy warheads used in practice were forty pounds lighter than the real thing, and no one had thought to compensate for the change.

But there was some success. On 13 September 1914, just nine days after the sinking of *Pathfinder*, E9 sunk the elderly German cruiser, the *Hela*. She was of little military value but the German High Command, worried by submarine activity in an area much favoured for exercising, decided to withdraw several squadrons to the comparative safety of the Baltic. Thus, within a few weeks of the outbreak of war, both the British and German fleets had been forced to move by the uncertain threat of submarines. British submarines did have some success in the Baltic later on in the war, attacking both the German fleet and merchant ships carrying vital iron ore from Sweden to Germany. But their most famous exploits were in much warmer waters.

Turkey had joined the Central Powers late in October 1914. Ever since German warships had escaped from the Mediterranean into the Sea of Marmora in August, several Allied submarines had kept watch off the Dardanelles. But neither the Germans nor the Turkish fleet showed any signs of venturing westwards and so, bored by the inactivity, the mixed flotilla of French and British submarines asked for and received permission to go on the offensive. The plan was to enter the Straits of Chanak and attack some of Turkey's ageing battleships which had been positioned to guard the entrance to the Sea of Marmora.

It would be a dangerous operation; the Straits were narrow, full of mines, and had currents which nearly matched the submarines' own underwater speed. All the boats were old, obsolescent and in poor condition. In the end the opportunity was given to B11, which at least had just been fitted with new batteries. On 13 December Lt Norman Holbrook approached the treacherous Straits. He had no fewer than five rows of mines to avoid, and navigation was unaided by any charts. The strong currents made control of the submarine difficult, but he persevered, and finally saw his reward – the elderly Turkish battleship

Messoudieh. B11 fired a torpedo, which for once did not pass underneath its target. The stricken *Messoudieh* immediately opened fire at B11's periscope, as did every other craft in the vicinity. Holbrook did not wait to see whether the battleship needed another torpedo, but turned and headed back whence he came. It was a nightmare return journey which his crew of fifteen would never forget. Harried by gunfire every time the periscope was raised, pouring with sweat in the stuffy, tiny submarine (this was one of the original Holland-based designs), the battery near exhaustion and the compass useless, time and again it seemed they must pay for their impertinence. B11 grounded on sandbanks several times, but eight hours later reached the safety of the open sea. Holbrook received a Victoria Cross, the first awarded to a submariner.

Over the next few months it became obvious that the Dardanelles campaign depended largely on the ability of the Turks to supply their troops from Constantinople. There were two methods. One was overland, by camel and mule, the 100 miles taking seven days. The other, major, route was directly across the Sea of Marmora to the ports on the Gallipoli peninsula. The Straits of Chanak were too well mined and defended by shore batteries for surface ships to pass through, but if the old B11 had reached half-way up them, could a more modern submarine go the whole hog and break through into the Sea of Marmora? The general opinion of the submarine commanders and their superiors was no: the distance to be travelled underwater was thirty miles and the difficulties of navigation immense. But finally Lt Cdr Brodie, of E15, claimed that it could be done. He did not get very far. The mixture of salt and fresh water made depth-keeping a nightmare. He was swept off course and soon driven on to a sandbank – only to surface right under the guns of a Turkish fort. Their fire killed Brodie and put the submarine out of action.

The next to try was the Australian submarine AE2. She went aground more than once, but survived and even torpedoed a Turkish gunboat half-way up the Straits. Despite a wandering compass and a near-exhausted battery she reached the Sea of Marmora. Thus encouraged, Lt Cdr Boyle in E14 followed two days later, but two French submarines were lost trying the same passage. On 30 April the AE2 was lost, sunk by gunfire after losing control and surfacing. So E14 was on her own, the sole survivor of the original group of five. For the next three weeks Boyle created havoc in the Turkish forces, his most significant success being a troopship with 600 reinforcements and a battery of field guns for Gallipoli. After thirteen days all her torpedoes were spent but E14 was ordered to stay in the Sea of Marmora, since her very presence so restricted the Turkish fleet.

Boyle added a nice touch now; from an oil drum, a length of pipe and some canvas, he made a dummy gun to hide his lack of firepower.

Over the coming months there was always at least one submarine in the Sea of Marmora. The Turks were convinced that there were many more, and their supply lines were severely disrupted through actual sinkings and the lone raiders' deterrence value. The passage through the Straits of Chanak became even more hazardous in July 1915, when the Turks ran a steel net from one side to the other. The only solution was to run at it head on at full speed, and hope the submarine would burst through. 'At 8.30 am,' wrote one officer involved in this

E11 (*below*) receiving a hero's welcome after sinking the Turkish battleship *Babarousse Hairedine*. Judging by the state of the periscope (*left*) E11's return through the Straits of Chanak must have been interesting.

passage, 'the Captain brought the boat to twenty-five feet and made his final observation before going deep to break through the chain boom and net defence at Nagara Kalessi. Having put the vessel at right angles to . . . the net we went to eighty feet again and increased speed. At 8.47 am we struck the obstruction and were temporarily held up, the boat rising to sixty feet. Additional ballast was taken in to keep the boat down, and in a few seconds the net defence broke, cables passing overhead and along the starboard side with much jarring and scraping. By 8.48, after one minute's excitement, all was peace again, and the trim of the boat corrected.'

Unfortunately, despite the success of the submarines in the Dardanelles, the campaign was ultimately a failure. However, the Army's Commander-in-Chief at Gallipoli, General Sir Ian Hamilton, admitted that one submarine was 'worth an Army Corps'.

Back in Europe, the opening months of 1915 saw a marked change in naval warfare. Fisher had declared the entire North Sea a military area and greatly increased the effectiveness of the blockade on Germany's ports. This in turn inevitably led to the German High Command resolving to turn the tables on Britain and starve their enemy out. There was only one way to do it, and that was to strike at the essential life-blood of Britain's war effort – the constant stream of supplies that arrived every day from all over the world by merchant ships. The obvious tool was the U-boat. The Kaiser was told that such action would force Britain to relinquish her own blockade of Germany within six weeks, and he accordingly authorised the campaign to begin on 22 February.

It was a decision which was to have fatal consequences for Germany. By declaring unrestricted warfare on any merchant ships bound for Britain, including, under some circumstances, those with neutral flags, the Kaiser risked affronting other countries whose ships might be attacked. He was careful to instruct his submarine commanders, in whose youthful hands many important decisions would lie, that they should be particularly careful to avoid sinking Italian or American steamers; but at the same time he signalled to them, 'If in spite of the exercise of great care mistakes should be made, the commander will not be made responsible.'

In fact, the German Navy simply did not have enough submarines to mount an effective blockade. At least three boats were needed to keep one permanently on station – a costly exercise. In February 1915, there were just twenty-one U-boats available in the North Sea. Attacks on merchant ships began sporadically, and during March only twenty-eight ships were sunk out of at least 4000 sailings from or to British ports. Ships' masters were advised to outrun the submarines if they could – or to turn straight towards them, forcing the submarine to dive (see p. 136). They were reminded that 'no British vessel should ever easily surrender . . . but do her utmost to escape'.

April was an even better month for Britain – only 50,000 tons sunk, less than half the March figure. However, the indirect impact of the campaign was considerable. Searching for U-boats tied up a great number of patrol craft, both large and small; everything was press-ganged into service, from armed yachts to destroyers. Anti-submarine warfare techniques simply did not exist: depth-charges had not been invented, let alone listening devices or sonar. A submarine was undetectable while it remained deep – although of course it could only move slowly and not for very long. The only method of attack was by gunfire or ramming.

May started ominously, with an attack on the American tanker *Gulflight* on the first day of the month. On that same day the *Lusitania* left New York bound for Liverpool. Five days later she was within 300 miles of the Irish coast. Much closer in, just twenty miles off Waterford, Lt Cdr Schwieger, captain of the U20, stopped the liner *Candidate* with the intention of sinking her.

Of the young U-boat commanders who fought this war, some were punctiliously correct in their treatment of merchant ships and allowed the crews time to disembark into boats before scuttling the ships. Others were less scrupulous; Schwieger, for instance, had four months earlier sunk a 12,000-ton hospital ship, the *Asturias*, despite the very obvious red crosses painted on her side. On 6 May, however, his conduct towards the *Candidate* was quite correct. But in the process of searching her while her passengers clambered into the boats, Schwieger's men discovered a machine gun and a six-pounder, both disguised. Any arming of merchant ships immediately disqualified them from special treatment by the U-boats, so when Schwieger came across *Candidate*'s sister ship a few hours later, he took no chances. The *Centurion* was torpedoed without warning.

By now, the *Lusitania* was approaching the Irish coast. News of Schwieger's activity, along with sightings of other U-boats in the area, had been transmitted to the *Lusitania*. However, no one, including her Master, believed that such a large and easily recognisable ship would ever be attacked. On the afternoon of 7 May Schwieger was advised by his lookout that a large four-funnelled ship was coming over the horizon. At 3.10 pm he torpedoed her. She sank within twenty minutes 1198 men, women and children were lost.

Much has been written about the sinking of the *Lusitania*. Was she carrying arms and explosives for Britain, for instance? Quite possibly

HOW to AVOID the SUBMARINE PIRATE

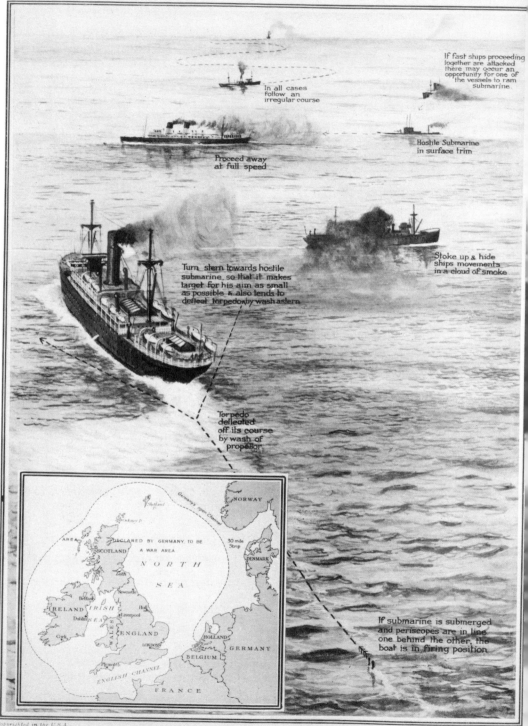

If fast ships proceeding together are attacked there may occur an opportunity for one of the vessels to ram submarine.

In all cases follow an irregular course

Hostile Submarine in surface trim

Proceed away at full speed

Turn stern towards hostile submarine so that it makes target for his aim as small as possible & also tends to deflect torpedo by wash astern

Stoke up & hide ships movements in a cloud of smoke

Torpedo deflected off its course by wash of propellor

If submarine is submerged and periscopes are in line one behind the other, the boat is in firing position

Shetland I.

Germany's open Channel

NORWAY

AREA

Orkney I.

Scotland

DECLARED BY GERMANY TO BE A WAR AREA

30 mile Strip

DENMARK

N O R T H
S E A

Leith

Newcastle

Belfast

Hull

IRELAND *IRISH*
Dublin Liverpool

SEA

Cork

WALES ENGLAND

London

HOLLAND

GERMANY

BELGIUM

Plymouth

ENGLISH CHANNEL

F R A N C E

DRAWN BY G. H. DAVIS

THE ADVANTAGE OF SHOWING A CLEAN PAIR OF HEELS AND OTHER DEVICES FOR CHECKMATING THE SUBMARINE

NOTICE!

TRAVELLERS intending to embark on the Atlantic voyage are reminded that a state of war exists between Germany and her allies and Great Britain and her allies; that the zone of war includes the waters adjacent to the British Isles; that, in accordance with formal notice given by the Imperial German Government, vessels flying the flag of Great Britain, or of any of her allies, are liable to destruction in those waters and that travellers sailing in the war zone on ships of Great Britain or her allies do so at their own risk.

IMPERIAL GERMAN EMBASSY
WASHINGTON, D. C., APRIL 22, 1915.

Left The warning that appeared in American newspapers shortly before the *Lusitania* (*below*) was sunk by Lt Cdr Schwieger (*inset*).

Opposite page Tips for avoiding 'the submarine pirate'.

she was, but there was no way that Schwieger could know that. One justification for his apparently heartless action was that, with the experience of the *Candidate* still fresh in his mind, he thought the *Lusitania* was armed. True, she had been designed with facilities to mount guns (although none were fitted) and she was featured in the current *Jane's Fighting Ships*, then as now an invaluable source of information for submariners. True, there had been fog in the area and this, coupled with a fortuitous turn towards the submarine, which in fact brought the liner within range, could have persuaded Schwieger that this huge grey monster emerging from the misty distance was trying to attack him. But it is all rather far-fetched. The truth is probably that Schwieger knew that the only way to sink the *Lusitania* was by torpedo. To surface and try and stop her was absurd, since with her speed of twenty-five knots she could escape all too easily – and anyway his paltry shells would take for ever to have any effect. If he was going to attack her, it had to be by torpedo and without warning. Schwieger's previous attitude towards the *Asturias* would explain his lack of concern about the consequences.

The sinking of the *Lusitania* naturally caused an outrage in America. But Germany stuck to her story that the passengers had been warned about the dangers before they left New York, which was true, and that the liner was really a heavily-armed cruiser, which was not.

U-boats continued to sink passenger ships and by now the campaign was becoming more effective. In May 106,000 tons of shipping were sunk, with similar figures for June and July. New measures were introduced to counter the threat. Merchant ships were given naval crews and disguised guns, and posed as live 'bait'. These 'Q' ships hoped to tempt the U-boats close enough to open fire themselves, and they did have some success. German attacks on fishing fleets had led to an even more bizarre trick. Trawlers apparently engaged in fishing would actually be towing behind them an ancient C-class submarine which, when the trawler was attacked by a U-boat, would in turn torpedo the intruder. It was a complicated ruse, and rather a passive form of anti-submarine warfare, but it did account for two U-boats in June and July.

But in the end the U-boat commanders defeated themselves. By continuing to sink obviously innocent passenger steamers they increasingly upset the Americans, who in turn threatened the German High Command with even more dire reprisals. The torpedoing of the liner *Arabic* on 21 August brought the Americans to fever pitch; six days later the Kaiser personally ordered that in future no ships were to be sunk without warning, and no passenger steamers were to be sunk at all. With the threat of the 'Q' ships, this was tantamount to calling off the campaign.

Over the next eight months the U-boat commanders must have wondered who was in charge. There were endless disagreements between the politicians and the military about the wisdom of returning to an unrestricted campaign. The Kaiser counselled

The innocent-looking 'Q' ships (*top*) took U-boats by surprise. Their carefully concealed 4-inch guns were disguised by false hatches and dummy lifeboats (*middle*). Their naval crews were disguised too; Lt Cdr Auten (*left*) seems to relish wearing his tramp skipper outfit.

caution, fearful of the political consequences; the Navy, backed by an Army commander frustrated by the stalemate of trench warfare, pushed hard. They claimed that Britain would be defeated, not within six weeks as had been predicted a year earlier, but within six months. When the Americans protested to Britain about the arming of merchant ships, the hawks in Germany tried to press home this political advantage. All it led to was a series of conflicting orders. On 29 February 1916 the U-boat commanders were told they could attack merchant ships and passenger steamers without warning as long as their armament was clearly visible – not so easy to see through a periscope at torpedo-firing range. A few days later, passenger ships were exempted. Then, on 4 March, the Kaiser finally consented to an unrestricted campaign, to start on 1 April. The U-boat commanders broke out the champagne, but that date should have warned them; two days later the Kaiser changed his mind. The compromise, on 13 March, was that they were free to sink all British ships in the war zone, whether or not they were armed, with the exception of passenger ships.

This constant changing of the rules of engagement must have been confusing and frustrating for the U-boat commanders. Stuck in their dirty, noisy, uncomfortable steel tubes for three weeks at a time, the only thing that kept them going was success. Thus it was perhaps not too surprising that the ever-changing rules were sometimes broken. The worst case was the torpedoing of the passenger steamer *Sussex* as she was running between Folkestone and Dieppe. Fifty lives were lost, including some American. Brushing aside the U-boat commander's lame excuse that he thought she was a troopship, America protested very strongly, threatening one month later to break off diplomatic relations. The very next day those long-suffering commanders received the latest order, and it was not to their taste: they must stop and search all vessels before sinking, in accordance with international law. With the majority of British merchant ships now armed, this was clearly impossible, and a few days later the final order in their campaign arrived: Return to base.

Over the next few months U-boats continued to harass and sink merchant ships in the Mediterranean, but in the North Atlantic their role was limited. The German High Seas Fleet had been bottled up in port for most of the war, but Admiral Scheer, who had taken over command in January 1916, had other plans. Now that submarines were available, he determined to involve them in his complex plans for raids on the east coast of Britain, and for other naval engagements. The submarines proved inadequate in this role. Their poor communication and slow speed made them unsuitable for working with the fast-moving fleet. In the Battle of Jutland, in May, the sixteen U-boats present had absolutely no effect on the outcome.

Three months later, Scheer decided to make another attempt to entice the British fleet into action, through a planned raid on Sunderland. British Naval Intelligence intercepted a signal on 18 August which suggested that Scheer was about to sail. Immediately the Grand Fleet under Admiral Jellicoe left Scapa Flow and Rosyth and headed south, hoping to surprise the enemy. The next morning one of the battle-cruisers scouting ahead of the Grand Fleet, HMS

Much of the Allied merchant shipping that fell victim to U-boats in the First World War was sunk by gunfire (*left*): torpedoes (*below*, in a painting by Felix Schwormstädt) were kept for the big targets but often failed to explode.

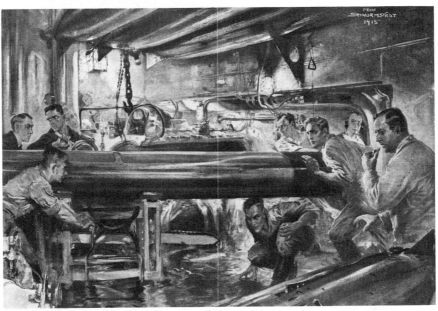

Left In March 1916, the passenger steamer *Sussex* was sunk in broad daylight by a U-boat, whose captain claimed he had mistaken her for a troopship. The cartoonist of the Philadelphia *Record* was sceptical.

Nottingham, was torpedoed by U52. She did not sink, and could not tell whether she had been hit by torpedo or had struck a mine, but she radioed to Jellicoe who without hesitation turned back. The mere possibility of submarines thirty miles ahead was enough. The German fleet was then reported 170 miles to the south-east and closing. Jellicoe turned back southwards, giving the area where the *Nottingham* had been attacked a wide berth. He raced towards the German fleet, convinced that a major battle was just over the horizon. But it was not to be. U53 sighted the Grand Fleet – the smoke from their straining boilers could be seen for miles – and advised his masters of the threat. Scheer immediately turned away. Jellicoe continued the chase, but soon afterwards the advance cruisers reported submarines. Jellicoe realised that he had been led into a trap, and he too turned away and retreated. *Nottingham* had finally sunk, and *Falmouth* was torpedoed during the retreat. In turn, E23 had earlier sunk a German battleship, the *Westfalen*. Thus the operation ended with many of the significant decisions and the only casualties stemming from the presence of submarines.

The submarine threat clearly concerned Jellicoe deeply, so much so that a month later he decided that in future the Grand Fleet would not venture further south than 55°30′N, which is north of Sunderland, because of the known intensity of U-boats beyond that latitude. Jellicoe's decision effectively neutered the Grand Fleet, and admitted that it had lost control over half the North Sea and much of the British coastline. Again it was the uncertain *threat* of U-boats that prevailed. Shortly afterwards, the majority of the submarines were withdrawn to resume the campaign against merchant ships; but the Grand Fleet remained bottled up in the north.

British submarines were able to impose similar problems on the High Seas Fleet, which seldom ventured into the North Sea again. This stalemate at sea matched that on land. Across Europe the armies of Great Britain and France, Germany and her allies, were deep in the appalling carnage of the 'Great' war. Neither side had a significant advantage. Both might have settled for peace – but neither wanted to be seen to be asking for it.

In December 1916, Germany saved face by couching a peace note in very aggressive terms, daring the world to refuse them. Lloyd George obliged, and gave the German High Command the extra ammunition for which they had been searching and hoping. They pressed their claim that an unrestricted U-boat campaign on merchant ships could bring the war to a successful conclusion within six months, and swept aside the politicians' fears of tempting President Wilson into the war by insisting that it would all be over too soon for the Americans to make any difference. On 9 January 1917 the Kaiser gave in and authorised the resumption of unrestricted submarine warfare.

This time there were over 100 U-boats available for the campaign. They were bigger, stronger and had greater endurance. But with most British merchant ships now armed, the Germans had to rely more on the torpedo (which also had improved) than the gun. The effects were immediate and stunning. By the end of January nearly 200 ships totalling 300,000 tons had been sunk. The February figure rose to 250 ships and 450,000 tons, and March saw 330 ships totalling over 500,000 tons sink without trace. The high proportion of sinkings by torpedo, without warning, led to hundreds of deaths, but for the U-boat commanders it was a dream. Individuals could amass incredible tonnages on each trip – their average was ten ships per U-boat per month. They returned home after each patrol to a hero's welcome. Their effect reached beyond sheer sinkings; so many neutrals were being attacked that many ships refused to come near Britain, for fear of the consequences.

Anti-submarine warfare still had not developed into an effective science. Crude depth-charges had been invented, but so few were manufactured that escorts only had one each. Mines and barrages in the Dover Straits were virtually useless. Primitive hydrophones could only be used in calm waters with the ship's propellers stopped. Between January and March the Germans lost just nine U-boats.

The future would hold the key to the development of anti-submarine warfare techniques; but even in early 1917 there existed an idea which was worth 1000 depth-charges – the convoy. After all, battle fleets travelled 'in convoy', protecting each other by their very presence. Why not put the merchant ships together too? Guarded by destroyers, the group could proceed unthreatened by the dreaded submarine. But the official view was unenthusiastic. There aren't enough escorts to go round, ran the argument. Think of the delays in assembling the convoys – and the difficulties of merchant ships keeping station with each other. And worst of all – what would happen if a U-boat discovered a convoy? It would run amok. Putting all the eggs in one basket would only serve up a fatter target.

The fallacy of this last argument took a long time to be exposed. The convoy system makes the job of finding targets not easier, but more difficult. The Atlantic Ocean is a huge expanse and the U-boat lookout's range of view is only about ten miles. He is much more likely to spot one of, say, thirty-five ships scattered across the ocean than one compact group of thirty-five ships travelling together. A simple calculation shows that, travelling independently, each ship is surrounded by a circle of water with a radius of ten miles and an area of over 300 square miles, inside which the submarine lookout will spot his target. For thirty-five ships, that is a total area of over 10,000 square miles in which the U-boat could strike lucky.

But the same thirty-five ships clustered together in one convoy form a moving box measuring three miles by two miles. With the submarine lookout's range of ten miles, that makes an area twenty-three miles by twenty-two miles outside which the convoy will not be detected. So, in order to find his prey, the submarine commander must be inside one area of just 500 square miles, in an ocean containing millions of such blank, identical square miles.

But the simple calculations were not enough to convince the Admiralty – although in early 1917 there was even practical evidence that convoys worked. The scores of little colliers that supplied France with coal from Wales and the North-East suffered badly from U-boat attacks during 1916, and early in the following year, at France's request, they were organised into convoys. Even though their protection was only a few armed trawlers, the colliers became virtually immune from attack.

The Admiralty was still a long way from sanctioning the convoy technique when, on 6 April, America finally declared war on Germany. The Kaiser had been right; the political effects of the unrestricted campaign had been far-reaching. The question was whether the military view, that Britain could be starved out by June, was right too. U-boat sinkings were still rising fast. In April one ship in every four that left a British port was sunk before it could return. The tonnage replaced by new ships was small. Britain was by no means starving – conditions in Germany were rather worse at this time – but if these kinds of losses continued there was obviously a clear possibility that the war would be lost.

Despite the April losses, the Admiralty still clung to their rejection of the convoy system, preferring to concentrate on patrolling the wide expanse of ocean. However, for the Germans the supreme effort of putting every available U-boat to sea in April led to a slight falling off of boats available in May. On Lloyd George's personal insistence, the Admiralty organised an experimental convoy of sixteen merchant ships, to sail from Gibraltar on 10 May. Its protection was so modest – just two 'Q' ships and three armed yachts – that it is tempting to conclude that the Admiralty wanted it to fail. But it worked. The ships kept station well with each other, and although progress was slow, they arrived south of Ireland on 18 May unscathed. From there six destroyers took over, and the convoy reached its destination without any losses.

A U-boat leaves for patrol in April 1917, bedecked with garlands. In that month German submarines sunk 430 ships totalling 850,000 tons – the highest figure of either World War.

A U-boat on patrol in the Atlantic, 1917. It was essential to be attached by a lifeline on the bridge in rough weather.

Another significant factor in that convoy was the use of aircraft. Although still slow and unreliable, they were becoming of immense value in searching for submarines, and even on occasion bombing them. Although it was still only a paltry six, the Germans lost more U-boats in May than in any single month since the campaign had begun. May sinkings were down to 549,000 tons, but this was largely due to the fewer numbers of U-boats at sea. In June the total rose again to over 600,000 tons, but in July fell again to 492,000 tons.

The Germans had calculated that they needed to sink 600,000 tons of shipping per month in order to bring the war to an end in the promised six months. Their average after five months was well on

The convoy system, when it was finally adopted, cut merchant-ship sinkings dramatically.

target, but the war was far from over. They had correctly predicted the amount of tonnage they could sink in a month, but had seriously miscalculated the effect. For example, they had not anticipated the effects of the campaign on the neutrals. Obviously their hope had been that all neutral merchant shipping would be frightened away by the campaign, thereby depriving Britain of more tonnage. But although this was the case at the beginning of the campaign, pressure from Britain brought most of them back by July. In addition, although Britain lost over two million tons of shipping in this period, 1½ million were replaced. The Germans had acknowledged that half a million tons could be built in British shipyards, but they had hoped to scuttle the half-million tons of interned German shipping that fell into the Allies' hands, and they had not reckoned on the half-million tons the rest of the world contributed. Simple things like more efficient use of still-available ships, shorter turn-round times in port, and restricting imports to bare necessities, all served to upset the calculations upon which these assumptions were based.

But the failure of the six-month estimate did not mean that the Germans were about to call off the campaign. Quite the opposite; 120 U-boats were already under construction, and there were plans for over 100 more. The need to finish the war was not so pressing; German land successes in recent months allowed them to survive another winter. And so the war of attrition went on, both in the muddy trenches of Europe and in the cold waters of the Atlantic. The convoy system gradually developed, proving increasingly effective. Its success led to a marked reduction in sinkings in the Channel approaches, formerly a highly dangerous place for merchant ships. But total sinkings during August were still nearly 500,000 tons.

One of the contributors was the huge submarine U155, which displaced 1875 tons when submerged. Nearly twice the weight of a

The huge Deutschland-class mercantile submarines were given two
5.9-inch guns and proved effective U-boats.

conventional U-boat, U155 and her sisters were originally built as
cargo-carrying submarines to break the blockade on Germany. The
Deutschland class, as they were then known, made several successful
trips to America, carrying precious stones and dyes and returning
with zinc, copper, silver and nickel. These monsters were
subsequently given two 5.9-inch guns and sent to war. Their
endurance and roominess made them ideal for long patrols, and their
massive guns had greater range than most of the merchant ships they
attacked. They were successful: U155 sank nineteen ships totalling
53,000 tons in one long patrol in the summer of 1917. This patrol
actually lasted for 105 days – almost as long as *Warspite*'s recent
record-breaker. Compare the two: *Warspite* has unlimited fresh
water, refrigerated food, a clean, silent power plant and every
conceivable navigational aid. The Deutschland-class crew probably
spent their three-month patrol without taking a single shower, and
had their drinking water strictly rationed throughout; within a few
days of leaving port they would be living entirely on canned food.
With no organised on-board entertainment it must have been an
appallingly dull way of life. The only advantage U155 had over
Warspite was the freedom to stay on the surface for most of the time to
let the crew breathe fresh air and even take the occasional swim.

But for most U-boats the rich pickings were gone by the autumn of
1917. The ever-fewer merchant ships travelling alone were invariably
armed, so any U-boat lucky enough to find one had to use a precious
torpedo. If they happened to find a convoy – about as difficult as
finding a needle in a haystack – a surfaced attack with the gun was
obviously out of the question. The U-boat had two options: to carry
out a torpedo attack by day, submerged; or to wait until night when it
could surface and fire its torpedoes. With the latter the submarine had
the advantage of greater speed; convoys may not have been travelling

quickly but they were usually faster than the U-boats' sustainable underwater speed. Night also gave some protection against the most effective, but tardy, form of submarine detection – its torpedo tracks, caused by the bubbles of compressed air. As soon as a merchant ship in convoy was torpedoed, the escorts would race along the tracks and saturate the area with depth-charges, now fortunately in plentiful supply. With such crude aiming the submarines were seldom hit, but they only had one opportunity to fire at the convoy before fleeing. By the end of 1917, each U-boat was sinking on average only five ships per month; in April of that year the figure had been more than ten. U-boat losses steadily increased in the last six months, as the difficulty of finding convoys tempted commanders into better-protected coastal waters. Here mines, aircraft and patrols were abundant, and these submarines had to work extremely hard for their successes. Forty-six U-boats were sunk in this period, a record for the war.

Through the late autumn and winter the stalemate continued. Sinkings averaged 300,000 tons per month. Merchant tonnage could not be replaced at quite the same rate, but the difference was not having catastrophic effects. U-boat losses averaged seven per month, and indeed Germany was building submarines at a slightly greater rate, so her overall fleet was increasing. But it is one thing to replace a submarine, quite another to replace its crew. Many of the experienced men had been killed, and the quality of their replacements was variable. No longer was this a glamorous life of easy victories and highly-publicised homecomings. Now patrol meant a month of dodging mines and depth-charges, with the occasional hurried attack and a total of four or five kills at most. Under the conditions in which they lived, it is not surprising that crews and their commanders became disheartened, and consequently less bold. But they continued to fight right to the very end. Indeed, the British battleship *Britannia* was sunk by submarine on the day before the Armistice was signed. The German surface fleet, which had remained in port for much of the war, had been showing signs of discontent for over a year; by autumn 1918 it was nearly in open revolt. A final sortie to engage the British fleet planned for late October had to be called off at the last moment because the crews refused to undertake such a pointless and foolhardy mission. Despite their heavy losses, there was relatively little discontent amongst submariners – although they firmly believed, with some reason, that they had been fighting on behalf of the whole German Navy.

By the end of the war 5700 ships, totalling over eleven million tons, had been sunk by German submarines. Fewer than 200 U-boats had been destroyed, with the loss of 5000 officers and men. German High

Command claims that the submarine would finish the war in first weeks, then months, were in the end unfounded. But it was close. If it had not been for the abortive campaigns of 1915 and 1916, which prepared the Allies for the massive campaign of 1917, things might have been different. The submarine had extraordinarily far-reaching consequences in the war. Hundreds of British warships and patrol craft were tied up in anti-submarine work. The economies of Britain, America and other countries were stretched to the limits to cope with the depredations caused by the sinkings of so many merchant ships, and the need to replace them. All this was accomplished by a maximum total at any one time of 150 cheap, small U-boats each manned by just forty men. It is no wonder that the very first item on the Naval Armistice covered the surrender by Germany of all her U-boats.

And only twenty years before, John P. Holland was still having difficulty keeping his submarine below the surface.

The two mainstays of the British and German submarine fleets throughout the war, the U-boat 160 class and the British E class, were very similar. The virtues of both classes were reliability, strength and relative simplicity. Both sides had flirted with significantly different designs during the war – the German Deutschland class, for instance. In the United Kingdom, Admiral Jellicoe was firmly convinced in 1915 that there was a role for a 'Fleet' submarine – one that could work with the Grand Fleet and, therefore, keep up with it. There was only one way to move a submarine as fast as the fleet, and that was to use the same power supply: steam. So in 1915 the K-class submarine was commissioned. Three times as big as other British submarines, it boasted powerful steam turbines that propelled it on the surface at twenty-four knots – by far the fastest submarine that had ever been built. But in many ways it was a backward step: these boats were definitely submersibles, and qualified even less as true submarines than their predecessors. Their hull shape was designed for high-speed surface work (they looked like low-slung surface ships), which made their underwater handling characteristics poor. With their steam boilers, they took a minimum of five minutes to dive, and underwater they were no faster than conventional submarines.

Seventeen of these K boats were completed by 1917 and attached to the Grand Fleet at Rosyth. They joined the Fleet regularly on exercise, and were certainly able to keep up. It is a shame that there never was an opportunity to use them in the role that Jellicoe had conceived. The only battle in which they were involved was one the Navy would rather forget – the 'Battle of May Island'. In the dark of

The British K-class submarine was capable of 24 knots – on the surface. Shutting off its steam boiler made diving a clumsy and lengthy process.

31 January 1918, a large group of Grand Fleet warships left Rosyth to rendezvous with other units off Norway. Amongst them were several K boats which, like the rest of the fleet, were steaming at twenty knots, without lights, in close formation. Suddenly disaster struck. A stray fishing boat loomed out of the darkness in front of K14. The submarine's captain shouted for a sharp turn to port, whereupon the helm jammed. Out of control and tilting widely, K14 promptly smashed into K22, which was out of position. Both submarines were inextricably entangled, and as the crews desperately tried to separate them, the battle-cruisers thundered up behind. Unable to see the low-slung submarine, HMS *Inflexible* also hit the unfortunate K14. Meanwhile K17, who had turned round to help K14, was struck by the light cruiser *Fearless* and cut completely in half. *Fearless* was leading the second group of K-class submarines, which now had to take avoiding action. K4 turned away and stopped engines; K6 only turned away. Moments later she cut K4 in half. Two submarines and many lives lost, two more submarines and a light cruiser badly damaged: a haul the Germans would have been proud of.

With the war over, Britain's Admirals reverted to Earl St Vincent's attitude of a century before, and set about abolishing the weapon that threatened their maritime power. At the Washington conference of 1921, Britain tried to have submarines banned altogether, claiming that they could only be of value against merchant ships. Japan, Italy and France disagreed strongly, claiming that the submarine was a perfectly legitimate weapon against warships. They subconsciously invoked St Vincent by arguing that, since they had relatively weak battle fleets, they should compensate with a more powerful submarine fleet. America, who already had a large submarine fleet, was opposed to the British desire for total abolition, but would have agreed to some kind of limitation. In the end, despite considerable success made in limiting the size and number of battleships, the conference failed to limit submarines at all. The only concession Britain could squeeze out of the others was an agreement that submarines should not be used to attack commerce. But it was never properly clarified, and France refused to sign it.

In view of Britain's insistence in Washington that submarines should never be used against commerce, her commissioning at home, in the very same year, of the X1 submarine was strange. X1 was a huge submarine – the biggest that had ever been built. She displaced 3500 tons when submerged, had a crew of 110, four 5.2-inch guns and six torpedo tubes. What could this monster be used for? With her heavy guns she could fight destroyers, but her surface speed of only eighteen knots made her useless as a fleet submarine. Obviously too big for coastal work, her 12,000-mile range seemed to be the key to her role – a long-range commerce raider, the very use that the British had been condemning in Washington! In fact the Admiralty were guilty not of duplicity, but of confusion. X1 was certainly not intended as a commerce raider, but as a step towards a totally submersible fleet – without the necessary speed. In the event, X1 was never a success. Her engines constantly gave trouble and she spent most of her life under repair. In 1937 she was scrapped.

Another example of the Admiralty's convoluted thinking about submarines was the M class. Torpedoes were a constant source of trouble; at the end of the war they were unreliable, inaccurate at more than 1000 yards, and packed a rather tired punch. Admiral Fisher's early remark, 'Our torpedoes won't hit and when they do they have the effect of so much sawdust', was still all too valid. Back in 1915 the Submarine Development Committee had decided that the answer was a 'Monitor' submarine. The M class were big boats, boasting a huge, sixty-ton twelve-inch gun which could be loaded when the submarine was submerged. The idea was to approach the enemy warship at periscope depth, load the gun, surface, fire one shot, and then crash-dive – all in less than a minute. It seemed a lot of trouble for the sake of one round, but the Admiralty thought it was such a good idea that they immediately stopped all work on it for one year – in case Germany discovered the secret. However, M1 and M2 were completed by 1918, although they were never used operationally during the war. They handled surprisingly well: the huge battleship gun helped to push the submarine down as it crash-dived, but then its buoyancy soon braked the descent.

A few years later, another committee decision removed the twelve-inch gun from M2 and replaced it with a watertight hangar, catapult and seaplane. Obviously useful for reconnaissance, this idea did work in trials, with surfacing, catapulting and diving achieved in

The M class, another Admiralty folly; its huge, 12-inch gun (*above*) was replaced by a seaplane (*below*), which could not be retrieved from the sea.

five minutes. Unfortunately there was no provision for bringing the seaplane back on board at sea, so again the M boat's use was limited to one 'shot'. But the idea never caught on and M2 sank in 1932, with the loss of all sixty of her crew. When she was finally found in 100 feet of water, her hangar doors and the hatch leading into the conning tower were open, suggesting that she may have been swamped during a frenzied attempt to beat the launching record.

It would be unfair to paint too dismal a picture of the Admiralty's submarine development work in the years after the First World War. Apart from the eccentricities of K, M and X boats, much useful

The fore-ends of a British submarine between the wars.

evolutionary development was done through more conventional classes of submarines, extending range and reliability, and improving torpedoes – a much more sensible solution than submersible twelve-inch guns. But perhaps the most important steps forward were taken in anti-submarine warfare.

The first requirement was to find the submarine. Hydrophones, with their essentially passive principle of listening for submarine propeller noise, would always have limited value. The Allied Submarine Detection Investigation Committee lent its acronym to an invention brought to them by an American, Herbert Grove Dorsey. Asdic was the first effective underwater detection system. A short burst of high-frequency sound from the searching ship bounced off the submarine and returned to the ship. The range and bearing of the submarine could be established, and all the while the escort could be travelling at high speed (with hydrophones, the ship had to stop its own propellers). Asdic was probably the most significant development in submarine warfare between the wars. It was soon fitted to many surface ships and submarines. The Admiralty was convinced that this spelt the end of the submarine as a significant threat.

In the 1920s it looked for a while as if that threat would come from France. Their vociferous insistence at the Washington conference

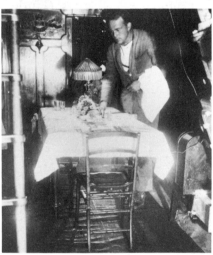

Living conditions on a British
L-class submarine between the
wars; the cooking facilities seem to
have become even cruder (*above*)
but in the wardroom (*left*) dinner is
still an occasion.

that they should be allowed to build up their submarine fleet; their
claim that it was they who had originally invented the whole concept
of commerce raiding by submarines, and their development of the
1000-ton Redoubtable class, highly suitable for sinking merchant
ships; their steady building programme in the 1920s, which led to the
largest submarine fleet in the world by 1930 – all led to growls of
suspicion at the traditional enemy across the Channel.

It was perhaps this strange obsession that obscured the real
submarine threat that was secretly developing in Europe. The Treaty
of Versailles had deprived Germany of anything more than token
armed forces, and forbidden her to own any submarines at all. The

effect on the Krupp industrial empire was catastrophic; for years this massive conglomerate had grown fat on arming Germany. Krupp was a far-sighted company, and realised that better times would come, when the restrictions might be lifted. When that moment arrived they were determined to be ready, and so, under the guise of a specially-created Dutch company, Krupp started to design U-boats. They sold the designs to Spain, Finland and Turkey, and indeed actually built some. The design was supervised by German naval personnel; the construction was observed by shipyard workers from Krupp in Germany; the exhaustive testing of the craft was carried out by German crews. Thus, when Hitler came to power in 1933, Krupp was ready. By the following year a total of twenty-six U-boats were laid down.

Hitler's repudiation of the Versailles Treaty in 1935 led to the Anglo-German Naval Agreement. In this generous document, Germany was allowed to build warships equivalent to 35 per cent of Britain's tonnage, but 45 per cent of her submarine numbers. (Under exceptional circumstances this could rise to 100 per cent.) The harsh severity of the Treaty of Versailles had swung the other way. But the British were convinced that with Asdic now fitted to half their destroyers and many of their submarines, and with depth-charges both powerful and plentiful, the submarine menace was illusory. Let Germany play with their new toys, was the feeling in the Admiralty; let them try to re-create the splendid days of 1917: it might even divert them from other more important efforts.

Germany knew about Asdic, but fortunately did not possess its secrets. What it did have up its sleeve was a new way of using the

By the time Hitler had been in power for a year, the Krupp Empire had already laid down twenty-six U-boats.

U-boats. Karl Doenitz had been a U-boat commander during the First World War. By 1935 he was running Germany's growing U-boat fleet, and soon afterwards he adopted new tactics for his submarines. He was convinced that the secret lay in grouping submarines together in large numbers. By attacking a convoy with several U-boats simultaneously, the confusion would be enormous and the escorts unable to cope. These 'wolf-packs' could hunt the oceans, ravaging convoys while they protected and supported each other.

By 1937 Doenitz was experimenting with the wolf-pack technique in the Baltic. The trials were successful. Doenitz estimated that 300 U-boats would be needed to defeat Britain: 100 at sea sinking convoys, 100 on passage, 100 in harbour repairing and preparing. By then Germany had about fifty U-boats, but there was no urgent building programme – partly because Doenitz had difficulty convincing his naval superiors that the way to defeat Britain was by what seemed to them to be a repeat of the unsuccessful campaign of the last war, and partly because Hitler's grand designs to build a navy capable of defeating Britain was a very long-term objective. The 'Z' plan did include orders for the necessary 230 submarines, but they and the surface warships were not planned for completion until the mid 1940s.

When Britain declared war on Germany on 3 September 1939, it was scarcely believable that, just twenty-one short years after the war to end all wars had finished, the soldiers, sailors and airmen of Europe were about to start all over again. The Second World War was, of course, totally different from its predecessor in a hundred different ways. The land battles in Europe were conducted at dizzying speeds compared to the earlier, static, attritional trench warfare; the use of aircraft, both fighters and bombers, transformed every aspect of the war on a scale undreamed of in 1918.

At sea, though, the parallels seem much closer. In 1939 the British were convinced, as they had been twenty-five years earlier, that the submarine was not a threat. This confidence was no longer based on vague notions about un-English weapons being no match for the finest fleet in the world, but on the more concrete evidence of Asdic and efficient depth-charges. In the event, Asdic proved a vitally useful tool in detection, but it did have limitations; and depth-charges are only efficient when they are dropped in the right place. Germany started the war still convinced that Britain's Achilles' heel lay in her dependence on imports, but again with insufficient U-boats to mount an effective campaign. Doenitz had 200 U-boats on order – but less than fifty ready for action, although this was at least more than the

British submarine fleet, which had steadily shrunk through the appeasement policies of the 1930s, and totalled a little over thirty in September 1939.

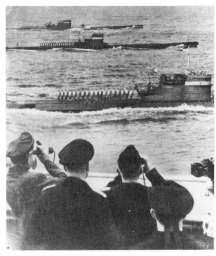

Left Doenitz watches a U-boat wolf-pack exercise in the Baltic.

Below World War II U-boats were bigger – but their bridges were just as exposed.

The submarines themselves were still similar, both to each other and to their predecessors. Average surface speeds were about thirteen knots for British submarines, and sixteen knots for the ocean-going Type VII U-boats. Underwater, both could manage about seven to eight knots. Range varied from the few hundred miles of the small Type II U-boat, used mainly in the North Sea, to the 8000 miles of the British 'T' class, a roomy, long-range boat designed for extended patrols in the Pacific Ocean. Armament had in theory improved, electric torpedoes replacing their compressed air-driven predecessors.

The visual similarity between the two sides' submarines – and indeed the inherent anonymity of the craft – led to some embarrassing and even tragic incidents in the early months of the war. In the autumn murk and stormy conditions of the North Sea the *Triton* mistook the *Oxley* for a U-boat and torpedoed her; only the Commanding Officer and one rating survived. Another hazard was from friendly aircraft. The submarines looked even more similar from the air, and aircrews had very little time to identify a sighting before, if it was a U-boat, it would dive and escape. There were many examples of British submarines being bombed by friendly aircraft, one of which led Lieutenant Gregory, returning from patrol in *Sturgeon*, to signal: 'Expect to arrive 2300 if friendly aircraft stop bombing me.' There was a certain justice in his misfortune: the *Sturgeon* had earlier narrowly missed sinking its sister submarine, the *Swordfish*. The difficulties of recognition persisted throughout the war; in all, five British and Allied submarines were to be sunk by their own forces.

The U-boats had their problems too. *Ark Royal* was extremely fortunate to survive when a salvo of torpedoes bounced harmlessly off her side. The Germans had endless trouble with their torpedoes' new magnetic firing pistol, which exploded directly beneath the steel hull. The degaussing, or demagnetising, of British ships, and the torpedoes' inherent unreliability, led to many frustrating failures for U-boat commanders.

But they did not always fail. The aircraft carrier *Courageous* was sunk in September with the loss of 518 men. However, Doenitz was convinced that it was possible to penetrate right into the British fleet's home base at Scapa Flow in the Orkneys. He entrusted this daring mission to Lt Cdr Gunther Prien of U47. It was clearly important to attack under cover of darkness, so on 13 October U47 lay on the bottom of the North Atlantic, just off the Orkneys, waiting for night to fall. The day had been specially chosen because of a new moon, in case U47 was unfortunate enough to encounter a clear sky. In the

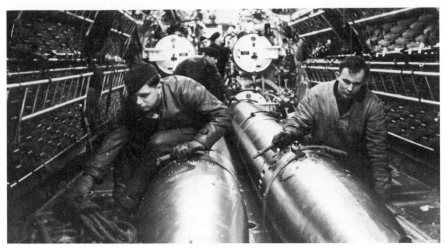

German torpedoes proved frustratingly unreliable at the beginning of World War II. Note the folded-up bunks at either side.

early evening, Prien gave the order to raise the periscope and, to his dismay, saw a sky at least as bright as one with a full moon. The aurora borealis was dancing and flashing above him, and its multicoloured display threatened to reveal his periscope to the multitude of lookouts he had to pass. However, they too must have been concentrating on the northern lights because Prien penetrated right into the enemy's lair and fired a salvo of four torpedoes at the battleship *Royal Oak*. One misfired, two missed and the fourth struck home but did only minor damage. Prien by this time had turned for home, expecting a maelstrom of depth-charging; but none came. No one on the *Royal Oak* understood what had happened; they certainly had no idea that a submarine had attacked them within Scapa Flow. Much to his surprise, Gunther Prien was able to turn back for a second bite at the cherry. Rapidly reloading the heavy, clumsy torpedoes – and praying that they would not fail – Prien aimed and fired again. This time there was a huge explosion and within thirteen minutes *Royal Oak* had sunk, taking with her twenty-four officers and 809 ratings.

It was a remarkable feat, and had as much psychological as tactical value. Prien returned home to a hero's welcome and received the Iron Cross; Doenitz was promoted to Rear-Admiral; and the British fleet had to leave Scapa Flow for safer anchorages further to the west.

There were other successes against British warships but, even though Doenitz was waiting for more U-boats to be built, he used what he had to attack commerce right from the start. On the very first day of the war the liner *Athenia* was sunk without warning. The

U-boat commander's lame excuse, that he thought it was a troopship, is reminiscent of the sinking of the *Sussex* in 1917. It was equally counterproductive. The *Sussex* brought the Americans into the war; the *Athenia* convinced Britain that an unrestricted campaign on all merchant shipping was about to be launched. Merchant ships were immediately organised into convoys, making the U-boat's task of attacking them much more difficult.

In 1939 there was much less *angst* in the German High Command about the wisdom of mounting a large-scale anti-commerce campaign than with the Kaiser twenty-five years earlier. Hitler started the war by publicly holding to international law, and in particular to the London Submarine Agreement of 1936. The British interpreted this to mean that merchant ships could only be sunk after being stopped and searched by the U-boats, and then only if 'contraband' was discovered. The German interpretation dwelt on the way the merchant ship was handled. They claimed that any defensive measure removed its immunity from surprise attack – and that 'defensive measure' included using radio, zigzagging or even running without lights at night. The campaign was soon unrestricted by the finer points of law, although Hitler had not given permission for U-boats to attack neutral ships.

Half-hearted attempts were made to form wolf-packs and attack convoys, but there were insufficient U-boats to execute the idea properly. Most attacks were made in daylight by individual U-boats against those individual merchant ships who were not in convoy. By March 1940 honours were about even: 222 Allied ships, totalling 765,000 tons, had been sunk, including some important warships; another 500,000 tons had been sunk by mines laid by U-boats. But the losses were balanced by new construction and the capture of German shipping. In the first seven months of the war eighteen U-boats were lost; only thirteen were commissioned, so although the British merchant fleet grew slightly, the U-boat fleet diminished by five.

The Battle of the Atlantic, as it was soon called, temporarily stopped in the spring of 1940 when most of the U-boats were transferred to the Norwegian coast to cover the German landings against attack by British warships. In the event they were totally unsuccessful. Despite twenty attacks on British warships, including four on the battleship *Warspite*, not one succeeded. Once again the reason was defective torpedoes, whose detonators were made even more than usually unreliable by the different magnetic forces in these high latitudes. British submarines had a marginally more effective campaign, but both surface fleets had one precious advantage that was almost as valuable as Asdic – the high latitudes' short summer nights. Submarines relied on darkness to allow them to surface and recharge their batteries; with only three hours of darkness a night, the very presence of escorts would often force them to withdraw from their patrol area.

As in the First World War, British submarines had their greatest success in the Mediterranean, although by very different methods. The Allies controlled the two ends of the Mediterranean, but enemy aircraft made the central section too difficult and dangerous for the British fleet to hold. Both Allied and Axis armies fighting the campaign in North Africa needed a constant stream of reinforcements and supplies. For the Allies, the route had to be the long but still relatively safe one around the Cape; for the Axis powers, the Italians mounted a succession of convoys across the Mediterranean to Tripoli, Benghazi and Tobruk.

Initially British submarines had a rough time. Between June and December 1940 they sank only nine ships, totalling 36,000 tons, which had absolutely no effect on the flow of supplies reaching North Africa. They also missed several Italian warships at point-blank range. Worst of all, nine British submarines were lost. Despite its friendly, warm image, the Mediterranean is a much more dangerous environment for submarines than the Atlantic. Its small size and the surrounding land make air surveillance much easier, and its limpid, translucent waters will not hide a submarine from the air when it is at periscope depth. The Italians had plenty of aircraft, so the British ultimately were forced into a method of operating their boats as very nearly true submarines.

They would stay submerged throughout the day; any surface running in light was suicidal. To avoid detection by aircraft and still keep track of enemy ships, they developed a porpoising system of patrol: ten minutes at 100 feet would be followed by a quick ascent to periscope depth, followed by another dive to 100 feet. Most attacks were made in daytime, submerged. At night the submarine would surface to charge its batteries, but would zigzag constantly to avoid attack by an enemy submarine. Wireless messages were kept to a minimum. It was a slow and cautious method, but ultimately it paid off. More and more supply ships were attacked until, by the Italian armistice in 1943, British submarines had sunk one million tons of Axis shipping. With the additional significant tonnage sunk by aircraft and mines, the effect on the convoys was such that Rommel was frequently short of fuel and supplies, which prevented him from taking the offensive. Forty-five British submarines were lost in the Mediterranean. It is very deep and, once it is damaged or gets out of control, a submarine will dive until the water pressure simply crushes it. There is little opportunity to rest on a shallow sea-bed and repair the damage.

In July 1940 Hitler removed the last restriction in the Atlantic campaign by allowing his submarines to attack neutral ships. Losses mounted sharply. Convoys were thinly protected by escorts, many of whom, in the summer of 1940, were patrolling the Channel waiting for an invasion. Individual U-boat commanders were notching up personal totals of over 100,000 tons each. By February 1941 U-boats had sunk 2¾ million tons of shipping which, when added to the 1½ million tons sunk by mines, surface raiders and aircraft, was starting to outstrip replacement. This was the so-called 'happy time' for U-boat commanders.

Their tactics were quite different from those of the British submarines in the Mediterranean. By now the wolf-pack concept was developing again. Five or six boats would make high-speed surface dashes towards the areas in which German intelligence had advised a convoy might be found. If they were right, the U-boats would drop back to the horizon, waiting for nightfall. Their low, grey hulls merged into the waves, whereas the high-sided merchant ships were silhouetted against the sky. If visibility was bad, they would use their hydrophones to find the noisy convoy's exact position. Hovering at the edge of the convoy escorts' Asdic range, they could even go to periscope depth and be fairly certain of not being detected; and they took care to operate beyond the range of Coastal Command's aircraft.

When night fell, the wolf-pack would speed up and, torpedoes loaded, head for their prey. Penetrating the convoy from five different angles simultaneously, they would cause havoc within minutes. Escorts would race around, dropping boats to pick up survivors or chasing dim shapes in the darkness. They had little information to go on; electric torpedoes no longer left tell-tale tracks of compressed-air bubbles, and the U-boats were fast enough to make their getaway on the surface. Unless a submarine dived and was picked up on Asdic, there was little chance of making contact. The truth is that, as Doenitz readily acknowledged, his U-boats were submersible torpedo boats and not true submarines at all. But they were nevertheless extremely effective.

It became a bitter, one-sided conflict in which the real heroes were the merchant seamen; men who had been sucked into the battle as innocent pawns in a dreadful game. Plodding along in their slow-moving, vulnerable ships, surrounded by the cold, grey, inhospitable Atlantic, they could do nothing but wait, hope and practise their lifeboat drill. For endless hours lookouts dutifully

Above Cause . . . and effect. Fourteen million tons of shipping were sunk by U-boats in World War II; 30,000 British Merchant Navy seamen lost their lives.

Left Searching for the convoy.

searched for the tell-tale signs of a distant hull or periscope. Dutifully, too, they zigzagged under the eagle eye of the busy, overstretched escorts, knowing that it would not do them much good – and was extending the length of the voyage. As the war developed, many of the seamen had seen other ships torpedoed, some had even suffered an attack themselves. Knowing what might happen made the passiveness of their role even more difficult to bear. As darkness fell, they knew exactly what to expect and could only wait for it: the sudden deafening explosion, the column of water shooting into the air, the violent shock of the stricken ship, water gushing in through the gaping hole, all seemed to happen simultaneously. Then, as men scrambled to lower the boats, some injured, others already dead in the bowels of the ship, there came the fear of a second attack. One torpedo was not always enough to sink the ship, and the fire that often broke out made it all too easy to hit again.

Sometimes it was a munitions ship, in which case no second attack was necessary if the cargo caught alight. The apocalyptic firework display illuminated the entire convoy and gave the crew no chance. Often the ship's fuel tanks were ruptured, and the black stinking oil spread quickly across the surface of the water. Sometimes it would catch fire, a blazing barrier through which escape was impossible. Even when it did not ignite, the oil was a foul menace. It made any pieces of timber or upturned boats too slippery to cling on to, and made survivors' eyes sting and water so badly that they felt blinded. Worst of all, it inevitably entered their lungs, where it caused excruciating pain and made breathing agony.

Other ships would be reluctant to come near their sinking comrades, fearful of presenting themselves as sitting targets, silhouetted against the burning victim. So help was not always quick in coming, and thousands of seamen spent agonising hours in the near-freezing water before slipping into unconsciousness and death.

For the U-boats, the major problem in the early stages of the war was quite simply discomfort. When they left port, they were packed with stores of every kind, to allow them as long a period at sea as possible. Passageways, messes, bunk-spaces were all piled high with boxes and tins of food and equipment. The limited number of bunks was still further reduced, and that traditional submarine practice of 'hot-bunking', whereby two men on different watches slept alternately in the same bunk, was commonplace. Spending so much time on the surface at high speed meant that their small, streamlined hulls rolled sickeningly for days on end. Continuously tossed around like so many tin cans, deafened by the hammering of the diesels, sickened by the smell of fuel oil, it was only the adrenalin of attack and the satisfaction of success that sustained the young submariners.

For the crews of the warships who searched for the U-boats, the major problem was frustration. They had neither the numbers nor the equipment to do the job properly. As often as not, after a day of anxious searching through binoculars for the tell-tale grey hull, they would watch helplessly as the invisible enemy decimated their convoy. If they were fortunate enough to force the submarine deep, they might pick it up on their crude and unreliable Asdic set, and then the hunt was on. But even then it was an uneven fight. One of the frustrating characteristics of the early Asdic sets was that they went completely blank at the most critical moment – just when the escort was on top of the submarine. Since the depth-charges were fired over the stern of the escort, just after it had passed over the submarine, this

Vice-Admiral Karl Doenitz in June 1941, at the height of the Battle of the Atlantic, with one of his U-boat captains, Lt Cdr Wohlfert.

Sleeping quarters in the fore-ends of a World War II U-boat (*below*) are no worse than in the British equivalent (*bottom*).

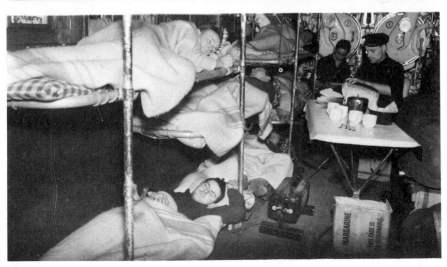

meant that the ship's captain had no precise knowledge of where the target was at the moment of attack.

For the submarine crew, an Asdic attack was a nerve-shattering experience. The tell-tale pings instantly told them they were under attack. Immediately the submarine would start twisting and turning, changing depth and speed and trying to evade its hunter. Often it would succeed, but with its limited underwater speed and restricted depth capability it was not easy. As the escort came closer, the volume and frequency of the pings would inexorably increase. By now the U-boat commander would have made his submarine as silent as possible to avoid the escort's hydrophones picking up any extra information on where he was; the submarine would be stopped, suspended in the water. Then, as the escort arrived directly overhead, the pings would stop. Knowing that the depth-charge attack was imminent, the commander could either sit tight and hope the depth-charges would miss, or he could exploit the temporary deafness of his enemy to move his submarine away.

In the event, only one in ten depth-charge attacks succeeded. Between June 1940 and February 1941 only four U-boats were destroyed by escorts. But at the beginning of 1941 a significant statistical change marked the first of two turning-points in the Battle of the Atlantic. Total tonnage sunk by the U-boats kept on rising, but the amount of ships sunk by each U-boat every month started to fall. At the beginning of 1941 it was over four; by the middle of the year it was half that figure. This meant that Germany could only sustain total sinkings by continuing increase in the number of U-boats at sea. Their accelerated building programme allowed them to do this, but the British anti-submarine effort was improving.

Churchill, who years later admitted that U-boats were the only thing that frightened him during the war, decreed in March 1941 that top priority must be given to winning the Battle of the Atlantic. Hundreds more escorts were coming into service, but sheer numbers were not enough; techniques had to improve as well. This soon became a fascinating battle of rival technologies.

The wolf-pack system required a tremendous amount of wireless traffic between the submarines and their land-based controllers, in which the latter would direct the wolf-pack towards likely hunting grounds. This traffic was intercepted by British listening stations, decoded and, as a result, convoys could be signalled to change course away from the U-boats. However, this traffic was also intercepted by the Germans and decoded, whereupon the U-boats were signalled updated instructions. And so it went on, a constant game of cat and mouse.

Apart from the gradually improving Asdic, a new submarine detection device was radar. Hitler had dismissed this invention as of no consequence at the beginning of the war. He had already come to regret his decision when the Battle of Britain had been won with the help of early radar warnings of approaching Luftwaffe aircraft. By late 1941 most ships and some aircraft had crude radar sets fitted; but their range, and their ability to separate a small submarine from the surrounding 'clutter' of waves, was limited. However, aircraft were playing a more and more important role in finding submarines, and their range was steadily extending westwards and southwards, in turn forcing the U-boats further from their bases.

By the end of 1941 these measures had reduced the shipping sunk per month to about 100,000 tons – one-third of the summer peak. Then, on 7 December 1941, the Japanese attacked Pearl Harbor and, four days later, Germany declared war on the United States. Doenitz was delighted; now his U-boats could have a go at the merchant traffic on the eastern seaboard of America. The only problem was range; it was theoretically right at the U-boats' limit. The solution was to pack in even more stores than usual and to save fuel by cutting down the cruising speed en route from Europe. This gave them about seven to ten days on patrol before they had to return. And what a golden opportunity it turned out to be. The Americans seemed to have learned nothing from the British convoy experience; their merchant ships sailed blithely on, lights blazing, radios constantly chattering, unescorted and not even in groups. They were sitting targets; the U-boat commanders, after their increasing struggles in the central Atlantic, could not believe their eyes. Attacking by night and resting on the bottom by day to conserve fuel, they sank no less than 300,000 tons by the end of January; in February it was 500,000 tons. American escorts were ill-equipped and undertrained in anti-submarine warfare, and had no experience of organising convoys. March and April continued at 500,000 tons each and the U-boat commanders talked of a second 'happy time'. Now Doenitz's new U-cruisers came into action. These were big 1600-ton submarines whose job was to carry 600 tons of spare fuel to replenish other U-boats at sea. These 'milch-cows', as they were nicknamed, had no torpedo tubes of their own, but simply a deck gun for self-defence. They greatly increased the efficiency of the U-boats by saving time-consuming trips across the Atlantic.

The destruction continued unabated. In the first seven months of 1942 3½ million tons of shipping were sunk, mostly in the western Atlantic, where just eleven U-boats were lost. Finally, in the summer of 1942, the Americans organised their convoys and escorts to such an extent that it was no longer worth the trouble of patrolling the distant eastern seaboard and the battle swung back to the central Atlantic.

Germany now had a total of 330 submarines. Of these 190 were tied up either in long-term repair or in trials and training; of the 140 operational boats, seventy were in harbour replenishing between patrols, twenty were on passage and fifty were on patrol – but only thirty of these were in the North Atlantic – just one-eleventh of Germany's total number. Against them, the British now had 400 escorts and 500 aircraft. With so many ships, it was becoming increasingly possible to locate and chase the submarines, thereby much increasing their fuel consumption; but still it was difficult to sink them, and the milch-cows took care of their empty tanks.

Aircraft were fitted with increasingly effective radar. Unknown to the Germans, the British had developed a 1.5-metre set which was light and compact enough to be carried on an aircraft and which could detect a surfaced submarine from several miles away. This was particularly useful at night or with low cloud, and throughout the early months of 1942 U-boat commanders were amazed to see aircraft diving through the cloud straight at them, dropping their bombs uncomfortably accurately. Their belief that the British had developed a new secret weapon was confirmed when at night an aircraft would emerge from nowhere and, at the last minute, transfix them with a bright searchlight before dropping its bombs.

The truth was that the 1.5-metre set had one disadvantage: rather like the Asdic, the image faded at the last moment. So at night a searchlight was aimed at the submarine, using the radar as a guide, and as the image faded the light was switched on – to reveal the surprised submarine. In the first few months of 1942 five U-boats were destroyed by aircraft using this method, three of them in the Bay of Biscay. But then the technical pendulum swung back. The Germans produced a search receiver, or radar-warning device, which could be mounted on the bridge of the submarine. Crude though it was, consisting of a wooden cross with a loop of wire around it, the 'Biscay Cross' worked, and gave a few precious minutes' warning – just time to crash-dive and escape. This technical war brought results very quickly. The first cross was installed in August 1942, and by October the air campaign had petered out.

So Allied losses continued upwards. Throughout the autumn and winter of 1942 and into the early months of 1943 the carnage was continuous. More and more U-boats came on stream, more than compensating for the increase in escorts and aircraft; still they could not be reliably found; still they could not easily be destroyed. It was stalemate, but the Allies were hanging on by the skin of their teeth.

Waiting for the invisible shadow in the water (*above*); continuous air cover (*below*) helped to swing the Battle of the Atlantic in early 1943.

Despite losing a total of 7¾ million tons of shipping since 1939, with the help of America they had replaced all but 750,000 tons, so their net loss was small and Britain was certainly not starving. But it was too finely balanced for comfort. Building at such a pace could not go on for ever; more and more U-boats were being completed and could tip the balance in Germany's favour at any time. Above all, thoughts of a sustained invasion of Europe were out of the question whilst so many supplies and troopships were in danger of being lost.

By March 1943 the Allies were desperate. Despite 500 escorts and 1100 aircraft in the Atlantic, the wolf-packs sunk 627,000 tons of shipping that month, one of the highest figures of the war. The whole convoy system was threatened. Then, abruptly, the tide turned.

With hindsight the reasons are clear; at the time the suddenness of the change took both sides by surprise. Since autumn 1942 the British had possessed a 10-cm radar set which was even better at detecting submarines on the surface and did not register on the Biscay Cross. But Bomber Command wanted the few available sets for its runs over Germany, and refused Coastal Command's requests. Finally, in March 1943, specially modified sets arrived. Unfortunately, one of these new sets soon fell into German hands after an aircraft carrying it was shot down. The Germans carefully examined the mysterious black box and questioned the pilot closely. After much stalling, he 'confessed' that the device simply picked up transmissions from their own Biscay Crosses and that, if they were to put those away, their problems would be over. His ingenious story seems to have been at least partially accepted, because work on a detection device for 10-cm radar did not start until 1944.

Also in March the gradual diminishing of the 'air gap' – the section in mid-Atlantic which was out of range for aircraft from either Britain or America – was completed. It had steadily shrunk as Liberators and Wellingtons were fitted with longer-range fuel tanks; now there was nowhere U-boats could make surface passage safely. A third major change was that sufficient escorts became available to create special support groups. These roving firemen, independent of convoys, could be used exclusively to chase and attack U-boats. The breaking of German codes – and improved cryptography allowing British signals to remain secure – enabled the Admiralty to guide these support groups towards the wolf-packs.

In April, all these measures began to bite. U-boats sank only half the amount of ships they had disposed of in March, but they lost twice as many of their own number. Now that the technology was against them, the pendulum swung quickly. May was disastrous: forty-one U-boats were lost, and on 24 May Doenitz had to order the withdrawal of all U-boats from the North Atlantic. The Battle of the Atlantic was, quite suddenly, over.

The situation had changed so rapidly because the U-boats had finally been exposed as not submarines at all, but submersibles. They depended too heavily on being surface torpedo boats which could, if necessary, hide under the water. They needed their surface speed to chase the convoys; if they had stayed submerged they would have found it impossible to locate any targets in the open Atlantic. When attacked by escorts, their lack of underwater speed was fatal.

It was technology that exposed the weakness of the U-boat; and it was technology that Doenitz turned to in order to regain the initiative. The immediate short-term expedient was a device called the schnorkel. A retractable breathing-tube, it allowed the diesel engines to run while the boat was at periscope depth, sucking in fresh air and expelling the exhaust. It was a brilliant idea, originally conceived by the Dutch and indeed used by their submarines, one of which was captured by the Germans in 1940. It allowed the submarine to remain underwater; but it limited its speed to about five knots. More than that and the protruding tube and periscope were in danger of being damaged by water pressure.

The only way to solve the underwater-speed problem was by more fundamental ideas, and Germany had two new designs which, given a few more months, might have had a significant effect on the war.

The Type XXI was no submersible: streamlined and sleek, its natural habitat was underwater. Displacing 1600 tons, it had huge batteries which gave it a maximum underwater speed of no less than eighteen knots – more than double the standard U-boat's limit. With an improved schnorkel and a long range, this was very close to the true submarine. Doenitz was convinced of its value, and so too was Hitler; he initiated a priority building programme of twenty-two boats every month from the end of 1943.

The most revolutionary of all the new ideas was Professor Hellmuth Walther's notion of a submarine driven by a highly-concentrated form of hydrogen peroxide called Ingolin. This, in theory, would drive a submarine at twenty-five knots underwater, but Ingolin was dangerous to handle, extremely expensive, and in such short supply that the submarines would need alternative diesel engines and electric motors to get them to and from their patrol areas. With three separate propulsion systems and a highly volatile fuel on board, much development time was needed. In the event, no operational Walther boats were completed by 1945.

Three months after he had withdrawn his U-boats from the North Atlantic, Doenitz was sufficiently confident to send some of them back. Apart from the schnorkel, these submarines had a limited supply of a new acoustic homing torpedo which would be attracted to the target's noisy propeller. But these two devices were insufficient to change the balance. The schnorkel limited the submarine's speed so much that it took too long to reach mid-Atlantic where convoy protection was not so heavy; it was also an exhausting trip for the crew. The schnorkel had a flap valve which snapped shut whenever a wave covered the top of the pipe, stopping water from pouring down into the diesel engines, but the engines needed air from somewhere and so, for the few seconds it took the schnorkel to drain, they sucked air from the interior of the submarine, causing a violent change in pressure. The foul exhaust fumes also temporarily expelled into the hull made the crew cough and vomit. Long passages became an exhausting nightmare. The schnorkel did have value for slow-speed,

The schnorkel, which allowed U-boats to recharge their batteries without surfacing.

independent running in coastal waters, but even then the smoke expelled from the exhaust could give a U-boat's position away. The acoustic torpedo was easily defeated by the 'foxer', a device towed behind the escorts which made a great deal of noise. In any case, acoustic torpedoes were not popular with the U-boat crews; they had to dive sharply and shut off their motors as soon as it was fired, since it had an unfortunate habit of turning directly around and homing in on the U-boat's own propeller.

The return of the U-boats in the autumn of 1943 not only proved ineffective in terms of sinkings; it also led them straight into the clutches of the redoubtable Captain Walker. Walker was an obsessive submarine-hunter. From the very beginning he had been convinced that the only way to defeat the U-boats was by hunting them relentlessly with groups of small escorts such as corvettes or sloops, and by developing special tactics to overcome Asdic's limitiations. Finally, in 1943, he had his way, and his Second Escort Group, with its sloops *Starling*, *Kite*, *Woodcock*, *Woodpecker* and *Wild Goose*, started to exploit his ingenious 'creeping attacks'.

One escort's sole task would be to hold the U-boat on Asdic and position itself behind its stern. It would then guide a second escort, which did not use its Asdic, towards the U-boat until it was stationed overhead and in the correct position to fire its depth-charges. Two other escorts would follow, ready to pick the U-boat up if it turned away. For the U-boat these creeping attacks were unnerving: the abrupt ending of the Asdic pings had previously told them when the escort was directly overhead and about to drop its depth-charges; now the pings were continuous and the explosion, with the violent shaking of the submarine and as often as not the sudden, fatal inrush of water through the cracked hull, could come at any time.

Walker's tactics were successful. Between September 1943 and March 1944 his support group alone sank fourteen U-boats. Walker

At the end of the war, Germany had dozens of the new Type XXI and XXIII U-boats under construction.

himself died of a heart attack in July of that year, almost certainly the result of overwork. By then it was almost too easy for the escorts.

The rest of the story of U-boats in World War II is a sad one. The fight became increasingly unbalanced, and in every theatre they stood less and less chance of survival. There was no shortage of new submarines, but the crews that took them out became progressively younger and less experienced. Often their numbers were under strength; sometimes the commander, himself in his early twenties, was the only commissioned officer on the submarine. In the remaining months of the war the Germans struggled on in the Atlantic, around coastal waters and in distant 'soft spots' where protection was minimal. They managed to sink another 337 ships of 1.8 million tons. But this was only a fraction of their earlier successes, and no threat to the Allied war effort. No less than 534 U-boats were sunk in this period. As the fresh young crews set off on patrol, it became less and less likely that they would return.

The progress of the revolutionary Type XXI boat, and the smaller Type XXIII to be used for coastal work, had been badly delayed by Allied bombing of submarine pens and by air harassment of their sea trials. But by the beginning of 1945 the Type XXIII boats were coming into service. Indeed, one returned to the scene of the dreadful massacre of the K boats, May Island, and sank two ships. These submarines proved extremely difficult to find and attack. Their excellent underwater speed allowed them to sprint away from danger, and of the six patrols carried out by the Type XXIIIs all managed to return home safely – which in 1945 was an extraordinary statistic.

On 30 April 1945 the first ocean-going Type XXI boat, U2311, left for patrol. Within a few days it encountered a British anti-submarine escort group, and simply sped away from them unharmed. But then, on 4 May, Doenitz finally ordered the surrender of all U-boats. U2311's commander reluctantly accepted the order, only to come across another group of British destroyers escorting a cruiser en route to Norway. He could not resist the temptation of mounting a dummy attack; records show that the quiet-running U2311 came within 500 yards of the cruiser, which knew absolutely nothing about it.

But it was too late. For the second time in twenty years the submarine had been defeated as the principal threat to Britain. It is useful to compare some figures between the two wars. In World War I 373 U-boats sank eleven million tons at the expense of 178 of their number; thirty-two ships were sunk for every U-boat destroyed. In World War II 1162 U-boats destroyed fourteen million tons of shipping with the loss of 784 of their number; less than four merchant ships were sunk for each U-boat destroyed. The figures show that anti-submarine warfare came of age in the 1939–45 conflict; but what they do not reveal is that it only just happened in time. Speculation is dangerous, but it is worth considering, for instance, what the effect on the finely-balanced conflict would have been if Hitler had not spurned radar at the beginning of the war . . . if the *Athenia* had not been sunk and galvanised the Allies into action . . . if Hitler had not withdrawn too many U-boats from the Atlantic in the autumn of 1941 to use in the Mediterranean and elsewhere . . . if those revolutionary new U-boats had been ready six months earlier.

The precise answer is impossible to give, but with the huge ship-building capacity and programme of Britain and America, it would have required an extraordinary effort for the U-boats to have deprived Britain of so many supplies that surrender became inevitable. It would certainly have prolonged the war and delayed any Allied offensive; but more than that is doubtful. True, American submarines had had a decisive effect on the war in the East by mounting a similar campaign against Japan; but Japan's shipbuilding resources were only a fraction of the Western Allies'. But although it may be over-simplistic to assume that submarine warfare itself could have brought defeat to Britain, there is no question that, as a means of weakening an island nation, it was remarkably efficient.

After the war, the Admiralty's major concern was to develop the submarine both as a submarine-hunter in its own right and as a meaningful training tool for the Navy's surface and air anti-submarine forces. Both a Type XXI and a Walther hydrogen-peroxide boat had fallen into British hands after the surrender, and both were used as part of post-war development. The Type XXI was the basis for the new 'Porpoise' class of submarine, designed in the early 1950s. With its immediate successors, the 'Oberon' class, these submarines have formed the mainstay of the Royal Navy's conventional submarine fleet for the last thirty years. Fine submarines though they are, the fact that, on paper at least, their performance is no better than the Type XXIs can be seen either as a tribute to German design in the 1940s or as an indication of the theoretical limits of diesel-electric technology. The Royal Navy continues to keep faith with diesel-electric submarines; it has recently ordered the first of the new Vickers 2400 design which will be operational well into the next century.

In 1945 the Walther hydrogen-peroxide boat was renamed HMS *Meteorite* and used extensively for trials. Britain developed its own design of hydrogen-peroxide propulsion, and built two submarines to test it. HMS *Excalibur* and HMS *Explorer* were unarmed experimental submarines and both had particularly long periods of gestation. Ten years later *Explorer* was accepted for service; her top speed underwater was a remarkable twenty-five knots, but not sustainable for very long. Thereafter, nothing more was heard of hydrogen peroxide; the whole concept of the submarine had been transformed by the nuclear-power plant.

The hydrogen-peroxide driven HMS *Explorer*.

The first nuclear submarine was the USS *Nautilus*, completed in 1954. Here at last, with its high speed and unlimited endurance underwater, was a true submarine. Development of this new genre was rapid. In 1960 the USS *Triton* circumnavigated the world, without once breaking the surface, in just sixty days. In the same year the *George Washington* launched the first Polaris rocket, a solid-fuel, submarine-based nuclear missile which was to transform the concept of international warfare. This was the ultimate deterrent – a weapon of awesome power, constantly on the move, invisibly waiting to retaliate against any pre-emptive nuclear strike.

The British were initially not keen on Polaris. They preferred the Skybolt project, an airborne second-strike system to be carried in the new V-bomber force. But Skybolt threatened to be increasingly expensive, and so in the early 1960s the Polaris system was considered. It, too, looked frighteningly expensive, and so alternative ways of carrying the deterrent at sea were investigated. Large conventional submarines, for instance – but so many more would be needed to keep the deterrent permanently at sea that it would be no cheaper. Echoing the days of the 'Q' ship, it was even suggested that disguised merchantmen could carry the missiles. This bizarre idea presupposed that it would be possible to sustain their anonymity in the open atmosphere of peacetime.

If Britain were to retain an independent deterrent, there was really no alternative to Polaris submarines, and in 1967 the first was commissioned.

The first true submarine. The nuclear-powered USS *Nautilus*.

CHAPTER 4

Bomber

They say it is the taxi drivers in Helensburgh who know first. Extra journeys from the seaside town's imposing railway station to the base just five miles up the loch, carrying men whose conversation is even less explicit than most submariners'. Then there is the extra business at Helensburgh's hairdressers . . . children sense that something is in the wind, although their mothers try to hide it . . . dusters flick over shining clean table-tops . . . the grass gets mown just one more time in preparation.

Then, early one morning, a black shape appears at the end of the loch – more mysterious, even longer than other submarines. Agonisingly slowly it crawls up the loch, waves lapping at its unnaturally long, flat stern. Wives and children cluster on the bleak sea-shore, hunched against the biting wind but not feeling it. Arms wave excitedly to the pale figures on the bridge; eyes look deeper, calmer; relief wells up in throats and minds. Some release coloured balloons, which the wind snatches and dashes against the rocks before they can soar free. Others sheepishly swig a bottle of wine. HMS *Repulse*, one of the Royal Navy's four Polaris-missile-carrying submarines, is back from patrol.

Repulse has already spent the morning creeping up and down the loch at periscope depth in a series of carefully controlled passes. 'Noise-ranging' uses highly sensitive recording apparatus permanently placed on the loch bottom to ascertain whether the submarine's noise signature has changed since it left for patrol. The smallest alteration must be communicated to other NATO submarines who, if they come across *Repulse* on patrol, must be able to recognise her as friendly. And an increase in noise output must be traced and fixed immediately. The Navy goes to endless trouble to silence Polaris submarines: the tiniest nick in the propeller will be carefully repaired; all internal vibrating machinery is insulated from the hull by springs or rubber bearings; thick cladding covers the outside of the hull around the engine room.

'Day Zero' – the day of the submarine's return – is a closely guarded secret, known only to a handful of men until it becomes public knowledge forty-eight hours before docking. Obsessive secrecy surrounds everything to do with the 'bombers', as the Navy's casually crude slang describes them. Their every need is given top priority – spare parts flown across the Atlantic, extra personnel dragooned from elsewhere. Her Majesty's Submarines *Revenge, Resolution, Renown* and *Repulse* are all a little long in the tooth, but they are cocooned by all the care and protection that the Navy can lavish upon them.

One revictualling and repairing, one in transit and one on patrol is the normal cycle with Polaris submarines, just as it was with Doenitz's U-boats. The traditional principles of how many submarines are needed to keep one constantly on patrol apply in 1984 just as they did in 1914 and 1939. The only difference today is that, with the complexity of the modern nuclear-powered submarine, a lengthy period must be regularly allowed for expensive refits – hence the fourth Polaris submarine.

As *Repulse* approaches the jetty, a lone piper starts to play. The official welcome echoes around the green Scottish hills that surround Loch Long, rising above the rumble of the two tugs' engines that are gently nudging *Repulse* the last few feet to the dock. Tense faces on the bridge and the casing, pale and tired after their eight weeks without daylight, are concerned only with organising the tugs, securing the lines, fixing the gangway.

A group of ratings huddle together on the quay, laughing and joking but not quite hiding their apprehension. They are trainees about to join *Repulse*; for some it will be their first experience of a submarine. Immediately *Repulse* is secure, dozens of canvas bags full of confidential records of the patrol are carried into a waiting van. Then immediate stores like fresh milk and fruit go on, but soon afterwards the trainees can cross the gangway and squeeze down the circular access hatch.

The first thing to grasp about a Polaris submarine is its huge size. These leviathans are over 400 feet long and displace more than 7000 tons – bigger than a guided-missile destroyer, twice the size of a frigate, nearly ten times the size of the average World War II U-boat. On the surface, *Repulse* is like a whale: a long, rounded back moving lazily through the water, the rudder tail flicking from side to side. It is only out of the water in dry dock that its awesome size becomes clear. Three storeys high from keel to fin and longer than Wembley football pitch, each of the skewed blades on the huge single propeller is the length of a man.

HMS *Repulse* returning from patrol.

Inside, it is not difficult for the newcomer to get lost. With three deck levels, stairs, passageways and a rabbit warren of bunk-spaces, it is on a completely different scale even from *Warspite*. Senior and junior ratings each have separate dining and recreation rooms; the spacious wardroom is L-shaped, with a chintz-covered sofa and easy chairs grouped around a low coffee-table and a massive dining-table to one side. Library, medical room, missile compartment, missile control room and separate navigation room are all peculiar to these submarines.

Some trainees refuse to be impressed, precociously adopting the submariner's studied world-weariness; others acknowledge openly that it is an extraordinary environment. One in particular admits that it is a dream come true. 'I went on a submarine when I was small, and I always wanted to join the Navy as a submariner . . . I'm amazed at the size of her, compared to other submarines – she's got a lot of space, good bunks – I'm really looking forward to going to sea.'

But there are still six weeks to wait before *Repulse* returns to patrol, during which the submarine's systems will be checked and repaired, and it will undergo a complete crew change. To keep these expensive machines at sea for as much time as possible, while simultaneously preserving the sanity of the men who sail in them, each Polaris submarine has two complete crews of no less than 140 men: two captains, two coxswains, two of everything. The 'port' crew that has just returned from patrol will hand over the submarine to their counterparts in the 'starboard' crew, and will then have a few days' leave. For three weeks both crews will work together repairing any faults that their jointly-managed, elderly submarine has developed on patrol. When the submarine is ready to return to sea for working-up trials, the port crew will take three weeks' leave; by the time they return to base, *Repulse* will have sailed for patrol. While the submarine is away, they will train and prepare for the next patrol; in some cases they will be given a month on duty in the sunshine of Hong Kong or Gibraltar.

Within twenty-four hours of docking the two captains have formally exchanged command, and the submarine is swarming with extra personnel. The sixteen massive cantilevered hatches that run along the after-casing fit so snugly that they are barely visible to the casual glance; now each one is swung open to reveal a Polaris missile nestling inside. The jetty crane delicately lifts each one out and deposits it carefully on to a waiting truck, which takes it away for servicing, accompanied by a police escort.

Five weeks after *Repulse* docked, she cruises slowly down the loch again. A ten-day trial period at sea has been completed without any serious problems, and she is nearly ready for patrol. In the galley, a frenzy of chopping, slicing and whisking is producing a splendid spread of salads, cold meats, puddings and cream cakes. Bunks are tidied, clean shirts taken out of lockers, not-so-clean magazines tucked carefully away.

Today is Families' Day, an annual public relations event in which the crew's wives, girlfriends, mums, dads and children over fourteen are allowed to spend a day on the submarine.

It is a warm and sunny day, and the black back of *Repulse* contrasts strongly with the intense blue sky and the green hills behind. As the tender, full of women and children, chugs slowly out to the middle of the loch, the waiting submarine wallows quietly in the swell. Some have visited submarines before; for others this is the first time. Soon there are gasps of astonishment at its size. The Captain, Commander Mike Hawke, waves a cheery greeting from the bridge and busily supervises the tender's final approach. High-heeled shoes totter across the gangway, nervous faces giggle as they line up on the casing, tight skirts provoke knowing glances from sailors as the women clamber down through the hatch.

Inside the submarine, this usually ordered world turns to bedlam within minutes. The spacious control room is filled with proud officers and ratings explaining intricate details of periscopes, valve gear and navigation equipment to their baffled loved ones, who do their best to ask appropriate questions.

Mike Hawke bustles into the control room, picks up the main broadcast microphone and welcomes everyone on board. He looks every inch a Naval Captain; a lean, strong face with piercing blue eyes, his prematurely grey hair betraying the fact that, now in his early forties, he is one of the most experienced submarine captains. Energetic and voluble, Hawke is proud of his submarine and of his position, and is relishing the opportunity to show both off to their best advantage.

He clears a space around the periscope and swings it rapidly through 360°, although the submarine is still on the surface, and announces merrily that she will dive shortly. Eyes widen perceptibly and the faltering conversation makes his request for silence superfluous. As the submarine starts the agonisingly slow process of diving, and tilts very gently forward, a tangible feeling of relief spreads through the control room – it really is not as bad as they had feared. In fact it is quite an anticlimax. Apart from the gentle tilting, there is absolutely no effect on any of the senses: no change in noise, no portholes to watch the fish through, just a depth gauge which swings lazily round to seventy-five feet.

Now there is a queue for the periscope. Helping hands operate the elevation and magnification, and there are more gasps as the high-powered lens brings the side of the loch close to the submarine. The submarine is under the water, but no one can feel the difference. A group of excited wives admit their relief.

'You don't feel claustrophobic at all because there's so much happening, so much to see – you don't even think of the fact that there's so much water above you – that you're in a tin can, in effect.'

'That's right – I don't think claustrophobia is as big a problem as having to get on with the same group of men for eight weeks.'

In the rest of the submarine, the guided tours are still going on. In the torpedo space wives eye the sleek black cylinders with apprehension, as if they might go off at any moment. In the bunk spaces, girlfriends giggle and chide. In the ratings' mess and the wardroom those who have either done their tour or who are not interested settle down to drink and talk. In the dining-room, howls of laughter greet the salacious excesses of the junior ratings' favourite feature film.

The mood becomes more sober as the submarine returns to Faslane. Mike Hawke is the only man on board who knows the precise date of sailing, but it is no secret that it will be within about a week. For some this will be the last farewell before patrol. It has been a good day, one which proud fathers will relate for years to come, and which wives and children will remember in the weeks ahead. They will draw comfort from the mental picture it has given them of where their missing partner works, eats and sleeps.

So the goodbyes are special. There can be few separations quite like that of the Polaris submariner and his wife. The value of the craft as a deterrent depends entirely on its ability to go out on patrol on time, dive, and remain completely undetected for eight weeks. American Polaris submarines have been known to return early from patrol, but there are so many of them that one early return or unscheduled surfacing will not affect the overall submarine deterrent. But with the entire British deterrent often resting on one submarine at a time, there is no room for flexibility. If the submarine were to surface or even to transmit a wireless message, its cover would instantly be blown. So it does neither of those things.

Moreover, the part of the world it patrols is a closely guarded secret which the majority of the crew will never know. So a wife must accept that she cannot know when her husband will leave, where he has gone or when he will return. She will not hear from him while he is away. If the submarine sinks the first that anyone will know about it is when it fails to return from patrol. She must completely take over the reins of running the house and the family, the car, the mortgage and all the bills. Her responsibilities, less easy to define than her husband's, are also less easy to fulfil satisfactorily.

The next week is spent making final preparations and loading the huge amount of stores needed for patrol. A chain of ratings man-handles seventeen hundredweight of bacon, 1½ tons of beef, 600 lbs of lamb, 700 lbs of pork, 900 lbs of offal, 260 chickens, 300 lbs of fish, one mile of sausages, over two tons of vegetables, three tons of potatoes, 11,520 eggs, 1000 gallons of long-life milk and 1500 lbs of fifteen different kinds of cheese: enough to feed a family of four for 8½ years. The stores disappear into a dozen nooks and crannies, including the walk-in deep-freezes and a vegetable store tucked into the corner of 'Sherwood Forest', the huge compartment just in front of the engine room where the sixteen Polaris missile tubes nestle together in eight pairs.

Although the submarine is stored for a longer patrol than most U-boats ever did, there is no sign of food or equipment overflowing into the accommodation space. The only problem is with the beer which is stored in the senior ratings' mess – dozens of barrels are piled high, to be packed away or otherwise turned into seats in the next few days.

Then, nine days after Families' Day, at two o'clock in the afternoon, *Repulse* slips away from the jetty. This time there is no piper; the only ceremonial moment is when the submarine passes the ritual group of wives, waiting at the narrowest point in the channel to wave goodbye. On the bridge, Mike Hawke anxiously scans the hills, other shipping, anything he can find. He seems genuinely to believe that the spies are out looking for him.

'My preoccupation is to get HMS *Repulse* safely out of the loch, down the Clyde and into deep water. The need is to get underwater and away, to reduce the chance of anybody observing our performance.'

But is anyone likely so to do?

'Who is amongst all these houses around us, I ask myself – who is in that yacht that sails past? One's got to assume that there's someone. We're going to sea to support the government's deterrent policy, take HMS *Repulse* away into the oceans of the world and disappear. We'll listen out for information for us but we'll remain totally silent.'

Some Polaris Captains take their boats well out to sea before diving, but Hawke sees no reason to expose himself for any longer than is strictly necessary. So, when the Clyde has become wider but is still a long way from the open ocean, the ship's bell is removed from the fin, heads duck down and disappear from the bridge, the hatches clang shut for the last time. Plumes of spray jet vertically from the main vents, and the propeller kicks white foam as the submarine's tail rises fractionally. The sea glints on the waves that gently start to lap over the fore-casing. Soon just the fin is visible, ploughing through the water with its own bow-wave. Then it too disappears and there is nothing left but the choppy blue sea with the green Scottish hills behind. But *Repulse* is there – a periscope bobs up, checks and disappears again.

On board, there is a sense of relief. The rush and hassle of the last week are over; now the comforting routines can begin. The men are resigned to being shut in their luxurious prison for at least the next eight weeks. But there is one rating who, although he was part of the starboard crew for the last two patrols, has remained back at Faslane base. As he quietly packs his bags, strips his bed and gathers all his belongings together, Radio Operator Andy Lucas, 19, is glad that he will never go on *Repulse* again. He surrenders his bedding at the store, has his passes stamped, and sets off on his journey south. He too had always dreamt of being on submarines. The dream came true, and one year earlier he had become an eager trainee radio operator on *Repulse*.

But as soon as the first patrol started things started to go wrong. Noises that he was not used to, noises of machinery that he did not understand, noises that worried him. 'You'd ask what they were and what was happening, and you'd be told and your mind would be put at ease. If they weren't always the same you'd ask again what that noise was, and they'd say it was a certain piece of equipment starting off. You'd think well, it didn't make that sound last time. . . . So on my first patrol I made a mental note of all the noises to expect when things started and stopped, but then on the second patrol the noises were entirely different, and sometimes rather alarming as well. Some people didn't bother about it, just went back to sleep if they were in bed, but not me. I used to get up and check things to make sure everything was how it was meant to be. It began to be a bit of a strain, getting up all the time and checking things . . .'

Lucas is sitting on a rocky, empty beach, on the opposite side of the loch from the submarine base. In the wide open spaces he is relaxed. He thinks back again to the submarine. 'There was the whole aspect of being dived. It worried me. It got to the stage where I wanted to go out to sea on a submarine and sail on the surface all the time. It really did become an obsession – I just didn't want that submarine to go underwater.'

But of course it did. One of Lucas's jobs, as luck would have it, was to clean one of the smallest and most cramped parts of the submarine. The 'tower' is a cylindrical space about twelve feet high by four feet wide leading vertically up from the control room to the bridge. At its top there is a hatch, which is naturally kept shut when the submarine is dived on patrol; there is also another hatch at the bottom of the tower.

'Most of the time we're at sea the lower hatch is shut and clipped, but for cleaning, people had to go up it – well, person really, because it's only big enough for one. At the top you can hear the water flowing past outside and to my mind there was never a lot between me and that water. That wasn't too bad – but when you're cleaning round the bottom, at some stage or another you had to shut that lower hatch. That used to worry me, thinking as I worked my way down, round and round, getting lower – I've got to shut that hatch, and I'm going to be the one in here, and if something happens outside, like we're coming too close to a large tanker or something, then the people in the control room would clip that hatch shut, and I'd be stuck in here.'

The most unnerving symptoms of Lucas's neurosis would happen when he was in his bunk. 'I'd go to bed – there's not a lot of room, and with the curtains shut, it's pitch-black, totally pitch-black, you can't see a damned thing. I'd be asleep, and I'd have what's called a coffin dream, where you dream you're being buried alive – the coffin lid is covering you, and you panic because you're being lowered into the ground. A lot of people get coffin dreams on board, but I used to get four or five a week. It only lasts for thirty seconds, but I used to kick open the curtains, rip them down, anything as long as I saw light and heard noises. Then I felt happy again – phew, thank God that's over – it was a terrifying experience at the time. I tried my utmost to get used to it but I could never do it, never.'

Coffin dreams are not uncommon amongst submariners, but Lucas's condition is. Claustrophobia is extraordinarily rare in the submarine service, although it is occasionally tried as a method of leaving the service before the statutory five years have been worked. For Lucas, the final straw was a particularly unpleasant incident which he could not discuss, but which others have described. An inexperienced trainee mistakenly opened an incorrect valve, and the submarine temporarily went out of control. Diving steeply, at an angle of over thirty-five degrees, it headed straight for the bottom. Unable to brace themselves, men went sliding across the floor, crockery smashed, chairs piled high on each other. *Repulse* was finally brought under control only feet from the bottom. Lucas decided that he did not want that experience again, and resolved to leave the submarine service. After seeing the ship's doctor, the Captain and a naval psychiatrist, he was granted a transfer to General Service. Mike Hawke says that Lucas is only the second case he has come across in twenty years.

A Polaris patrol raises all kinds of 'what if' questions. What if someone becomes sick on patrol, or even dies? What if a wife or child gets seriously ill or dies? What if the submarine breaks down? And what, ultimately, if war breaks out and the order arrives to use the deterrent?

Polaris submarines are the only ones that always carry a doctor. Surgeon-Lieutenant Richard Garth on *Repulse* knows that for the first week of patrol he will have a flood of colds and sore throats to deal with. The closed cycle of the air-conditioning system ensures that any bug is circulated throughout the boat, so it only needs one sore throat on the day of sailing for a dozen or more to be affected soon afterwards. Garth does other watchkeeping duties too, and constantly tests the atmosphere to ensure that the electrolysers are keeping it in specification and that no radiation is leaking. But he is really there as an insurance policy to tackle medical emergencies. He can convert the senior ratings' dining hall into an operating theatre for minor operations such as appendectomies, but if possible he prefers to use medication just to keep the condition under control. The submarine is clean but it is by no means sterile, and the chances of infection are high. The technique has worked with appendixes; several times he has just used antibiotics on quite serious cases, which on land would have been operated on instantly. They have survived the patrol and gone straight into hospital on return.

The obvious question is: what happens if someone becomes very seriously ill and the ship's doctor cannot cope? Will the submarine surface to evacuate him, or remain operational and risk his life? The Navy refuses to say categorically what would happen, but claims that no Polaris submarine has ever had to return from patrol early, and that no one has died whilst on patrol. If someone were to die, incidentally, the question of disposal of the body arises. There is no opportunity for a traditional burial at sea, so the regulations say that the corpse must be put in the deep-freeze until return – having first removed the food. The truth is that every member of the crew is medically vetted with great care before sailing on patrol, and any suspect cases are just not allowed to come. Even a mild case of dermatitis was not allowed to come on this patrol; they take no chances.

The same goes for dental health; although one glance at Richard Garth's standard Naval dental kit would be sufficient to cure all but the worst toothache.

A few days after patrol starts, two women sit down to the first of several weekly rituals. Juliet Hawke has fed the ducks, taken her small son to school, and returned to her pretty white cottage set in the hillside overlooking the loch. She sits down in the kitchen, takes out an official naval form and pauses for thought. Dawn Saunders has packed her children off to the local school, dusted the furniture and hoovered the carpet of her bungalow in Helensburgh, and she too sits down at a table, lights a cigarette and stares at an identical form.

Although *Repulse* is forbidden to transmit any wireless messages, she must be able to receive them at all times – even when travelling at several hundred feet under the water. So for the entire patrol the submarine streams a long wire which floats up to the surface, and which will receive VLF (Very Low Frequency) radio transmissions.

Amongst the routine one-way traffic are the 'familygrams' – forty-word personal messages that each submariner is entitled to receive once a week from someone in his family. They are his one contact with home for the entire patrol.

Two of the precious forty words have to be squandered on name and rank; composing the remaining thirty-eight is an art. Juliet Hawke admits it is a difficult one. 'I don't think forty words is enough to tell Mike all that I want to tell him. You have to be very careful what you put. I wouldn't want to put anything that would worry him. I struggle each week at it, but I know he enjoys them when he gets them.'

For Dawn, the problem of what to say looms large. 'Sometimes I've sat here for an hour trying to find something to write. It's awkward because you want to tell him so much, but you have to be careful.

When Mark broke his arm I didn't tell John – I thought I'd wait until he came home and he could see the boy was OK. I just try and make it light, let him know I'm missing him, but not all lovey-dovey – especially since they read them in public.'

There is so much to pack in, so much that has happened, so much that the sender wants to say; yet she has to be so careful not to sow seeds of doubt in the submariner's mind. He will read the tiny slips of paper over and over again, savouring everything positive, worrying away at the ambiguous or problematical. It is important, for instance, not to mention a visit to the doctor without giving the result; it simply means a week of worry for the husband. Even small problems can loom large when there is nothing that can be done to solve them; so today Dawn is wrestling with a form of words which will wittily tell her husband that the lawn mower has broken: 'Saunders MEM 1. No domestic disasters this week, except mower blew up. Spacers found in pocket, too late, Dad got mower first. Lawn looks nice, roses died in amazement. Having birthday party with 16 assorted brats; big headache. Love Dawn.'

Juliet's familygram is a classic example of the delicate art of familygram writing. In the last week one daughter has been in hospital, one returned to boarding school, and the local elements have run riot; but she combines information with reassurance in every case: 'Hawke, Commander. Tonsils, adenoids out, Rachel fine, just off to see her. Trunk gone, heavy storm weekend, house fine. Katy's first riding lesson great success. Sam delighted to be back at school, no problems here. All miss you. Love Jules.'

So on top of the responsibility of paying the bills and managing the family, the wives must protect their husbands from any problems. They cannot share their cares; quite the opposite, they must deliberately keep them to themselves.

On the submarine, familygrams are distributed outside the wireless office. Most men receive theirs on a regular day each week, and the summons comes as a relief. The sheer fact of it arriving is in itself a comfort and reassurance. But once the pleasure of receiving them is over, the actual content can be a disappointment.

'We tend to call them "grumbly grams",' admits Dawn's husband John, as he sits with his precious scrap of paper in the senior ratings' mess. 'Every time you get them the wives tend to be grumbling about the kids, the weather or something else insignificant. But the old grumblies are important to us and we look forward to getting them.'

But there is one thing about the familygram which directly reflects the difference between a Polaris submariner and any other sailor. 'Sometimes I think it would be better not to get them at all, because when they're late you tend to think all sorts of things, wondering about what your wife's up to.' Secure in the knowledge that her husband is effectively in an all-male prison for two months, the one absolute assurance the wife has is that of fidelity. But the husband has no such guarantee.

Dawn smiles quietly at the thought. 'Some husbands do worry about their wives. I know he worries that we're all OK, but I know he doesn't worry about whether I'm going to be here when he comes home. I know he trusts me completely and he knows that I'll always be here waiting for him.'

For Mike Hawke, the personal pleasure of receiving news about the family from Juliet is sometimes tempered by the need to perpetuate an elaborate ritual with one of his crew's familygrams. Before going on patrol, every member of the crew has to state how he wants to receive news of a death or an accident in the family. He has three options about when to be told: immediately, on return from patrol, or twenty-four hours before docking. The vast majority choose the last option, preferring to remain in ignorance while on patrol rather than experience the frustration of not being able to help the family. John Saunders is one. 'If any bad news happens, I just don't want to know about it. I don't want to be stuck down here thinking about it for six weeks. There's nothing I can do about it, so I wouldn't want to know until I came up.'

If a serious tragedy does occur within the family of one of the crew, the Navy will keep such information out of the familygram, either by direct editing or by agreeing how to rewrite it with the sender. Direct editing is unwise – it leads to a familygram of less than forty words, which in itself is so unusual that it will raise suspicion in the recipient's mind; and even extra phrases to replace the missing words can lead to trouble. One rating remembers the time when, while he was on patrol, his two-month-old daughter had to be taken into hospital. His wife mentioned this in the familygram, but the Navy chose to take it out and replace the words with a phrase about the weather. However, their editing was clumsy, and the familygram read: 'Have taken Sarah to the doctor, the weather is fine.'

'Now, the one thing I'd impressed on my wife was – everybody knows what the weather is like, so don't even mention it. That familygram just didn't ring true. It was three weeks into patrol, and for the next five weeks I knew something was wrong but I didn't know what. Was Sarah at home? Was she mentioned? It was a huge worry. Fortunately she was all right.'

Hawke is immediately informed of the home problem and it is his unpleasant task to convey the bad news as the patrol draws to an end.

HMS *Repulse* moving down the Clyde on her way to patrol. One of the Royal Navy's four nuclear-powered Polaris submarines, *Repulse* is over 400 feet long, displaces more than 7000 tons, and has a crew of thirteen officers and 130 ratings. Under her long back are sixteen Polaris missiles.

Repulse at periscope depth. If she were on the surface, the submarine would fill the width of the photograph.

Overleaf 'Open main vents.' *Repulse* starts her last dive for at least eight weeks.

The control room of a Polaris submarine. The two planesmen control the submarine's depth and angle. Behind them sits the Ship Control Officer of the Watch, who relays depth and course change orders. For much of the patrol the submarine is on autopilot, set between the two planesmen.

The Missile Control Centre of a Polaris submarine. The officer in the foreground is holding the pistol-grip trigger which fires the missiles.

Left A Polaris submarine at Coulport Base, Loch Long, Scotland. A Polaris missile is carefully raised out of its tube to be taken away for servicing.

Checking samples for radioactivity in the Health Physics Laboratory.

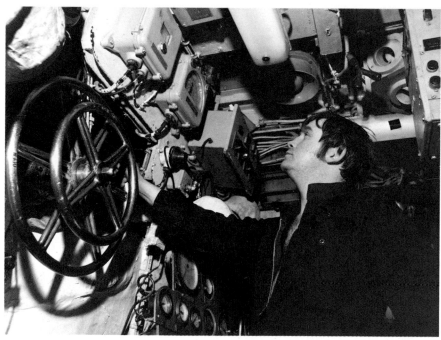

The main machinery space on a Polaris submarine. Despite their relative roominess, there are still many places that have the traditional cramped feeling of a submarine.

Much of a Polaris patrol is spent playing 'uckers', the naval version of Ludo.

When fully prepared for patrol, a Polaris submarine's stores will include three tons of meat, 11,500 eggs, and a mile of sausages – but the fresh fruit and vegetables will soon run out.

This practice makes the last twenty-four hours of patrol even more tense than they might otherwise be. Anyone who is unexpectedly summoned to the Captain's cabin is convinced he is about to be given some bad news. It can be all sorts of things from death to desertion. 'On my first patrol as Captain a man's son died within four days of us leaving. I was told about a week later, and I kept a close eye on his familygrams, to make sure no hint of it came through. His wife was remarkably courageous – there was no hint. I told him about three hours before we got back alongside. I don't find it the easiest thing to do, but it's something that has to happen.'

Familygrams become more important as the patrol goes on. As the submarine slips into its quiet, repetitive routine there is less to keep men's thoughts away from home, and that weekly message, however inadequate, is a lifeline to the real world. Over the weeks they collect the tiny slips of paper together into a brief but precious diary of the patrol, which gets read over and over again.

Repulse moves slowly and quietly on, seldom exceeding walking pace, hiding under the protecting layer of the ocean. She could be almost anywhere. The range of the Polaris missile is 2500 miles; there is an endless expanse of ocean in which to hide and still remain within 2500 miles of the Soviet Union. She could have been in the North Sea, the Arctic Ocean, the Barents Sea, the Baltic Sea, or the Eastern Atlantic. Less likely but still possible are the Mediterranean and the Arabian Seas, the Indian or the Pacific Oceans. It is perfectly possible, albeit unlikely, that she went no further than the Irish Sea – or even that she stayed in the Clyde and listened to the Perisher submarines and their busy frigates. Hardly anyone on board knows, and most don't care.

By mid-patrol, week 4, morale is beginning to flag a little. The Airfix models have been finished, no one wants to see yet another macramé owl, the best films have all been run, and the fresh food ran out long ago. Men are becoming tired of seeing the same faces every day, with the same irritating idiosyncrasies. The First Lieutenant arranges quizzes, competitions and social events, including an elaborate and noisy substitute for horse-racing. Apart from the familygram, the only contact with the outside world is a daily news sheet which is transmitted to all submarines: a brief digest of the news and sport usually taken from the *Daily Telegraph*, followed by a word game or crossword puzzle. But by and large there's not much to do except sleep, go on watch and eat. The cooks do their best to keep the food varied but it is an uphill struggle; their menu is governed by the order in which the food was loaded into the massive deep-freezes. They are the ones who can most closely observe the crew's everyday

Left Nowhere on earth is out of the 2500-mile range of the Polaris missile.

behaviour, as the men troop in to collect their breakfast, lunch and dinner.

'It starts off unsettled for the first week, until everyone gets into their routine. But then about week 5 they start geting a little bit edgy, because they've all done enough. Then about week 6 it all starts to happen. They start thinking about home and go into what we call a glaze. We stand in the galley and watch them. They'll sit there and half eat their meal, and then they'll just stare at the bulkhead – we know what they're thinking about, and it's dead funny – they'll sit there for ten, twenty minutes before they realise what they're doing.'

The cooks have developed their own reminder of the outside world; over the washing-up sink are a pair of net curtains, and pasted on to the wall between them is an impossibly bright photograph of the Scottish hills.

Other submariners' attitudes towards Polaris crews vary between officers and ratings. There is a certain disdain amongst the officers of diesel-electric and hunter-killer submarines; their feeling is that the Polaris patrol – eight weeks at walking pace – is no way for a keen submariner to behave. They claim to dread the boredom of it; but there is often a secret envy of the relative comfort. Ratings on other submarines are more openly envious of their Polaris counterparts. The great attraction for them – especially the older men with families – is the completely predictable and regular cycle of patrols. Submarines such as *Warspite* and *Oracle* have a very unpredictable operational life, having to snatch leave at the odd weekend or at short notice. Polaris submarines, with their two crews and fixed pattern of patrols, allow the submariner to arrange summer holidays, know when he will be away for Christmas, and generally plan his life.

'XO and WEO to the wireless office.' The crackling, urgent announcement sends Lieutenant Commanders David Southcott and Mike Reeves tumbling out of their bunks and racing up to the wireless room. There they are given a signal from the Prime Minister via the Navy's headquarters at Northwood which orders them to fire sixteen Polaris missiles at a precise target – for exercise only.

There are endless exercises on patrol, from fire-fighting to breakdown simulation; they keep training up to standard and they serve to fill in time. Every few days, at the whim of Northwood, *Repulse* is triggered into a missile-firing exercise. It is an elaborate procedure, designed for maximum protection against the possibility of sabotage or error, from inside the submarine or from where the message originates, but at the same time to provide a rapid response.

Being on exercise, it also contains a series of interlocking precautions designed to remove the possibility of an accidental firing. What follows therefore is a brief description of the procedure for what could be called 'the real thing'.

David Southcott, First Lieutenant, and Mike Reeves, Weapons Engineer Officer, go straight from the wireless room, through the control room, to the Nav-centre. Here the submarine's position is monitored, using an inertial-navigation system; access is restricted to the dozen or so members of the crew who have a need to know where *Repulse* is. In case an unauthorised person should accidentally, or by design, enter the Nav-centre, the charts are always kept upside down; in here, as in other key parts of the submarine related to its deterrent role, there are truncheons hanging. The ratings in each of these areas are fully authorised – and only too willing – to use them on any unauthorised person who tampers with key equipment.

The complex sequence of events must start with a check that the coded message from Northwood is valid. Reeves announces, 'Opening the safes,' and deliberately guides a rating away from where he is standing in full view of the combination lock. This is in fact a safe within a safe. The combination of the outer safe is known only to Mike Reeves and one other officer; the combination of the inner safe is known only to the Captain and the First Lieutenant. In each safe there is only half of the information needed to verify the firing signal.

Reeves and Southcott have taken out their verification cards, and check them against the signal. 'My half authenticates.' 'Authentification time?' '0840.' Reeves repeats the time and writes it down. They both replace their cards in the safes. 'Safes are shut,' announces Reeves. 'Let's go and see the captain.'

In the control room, the submarine has been brought to a near standstill. An officer stands at the control panel, checking trim and ballast. 'Test hover system valves.' John Saunders, sitting at the panel, repeats the order. The submarine must be suspended virtually motionless in the water when the missiles are fired. Polaris submarines therefore have a computerised system which finely controls several different hull valves, making minute adjustments of a few gallons of water to keep the submarine hovering.

Southcott and Reeves emerge from the Nav-centre, and Reeves announces to the waiting captain: 'Message authenticates, Sir.' 'Good. Set condition 1 SQ.' Southcott picks up the broadcast microphone. 'Set condition 1 SQ.' This is the order to bring the missiles to full readiness. Reeves sets off for the Missile Control Centre.

The MCC is filled with computerised equipment related to the missiles; Reeves strides in, and kneels down by another safe. It is another combination lock; behind him hangs another truncheon. Out of the safe he brings what looks like the butt of a Colt 45, with a lead which remains plugged into the back of the safe. It even has a red trigger.

In the control room, the Captain moves across to the control panel. 'Stand by to start hovering.' He checks the submarine's speed and depth. 'Stop engines. Start hovering.' John Saunders repeats the order. 'Hover hull-valve open . . . hovering in auto, computer one.'

In the MCC, the target information has been fed into the computers. Reeves waits whilst a rating performs multiple checks on the missiles. He presses sixteen different buttons and checks that each time a series of green displays illuminate, revealing that each missile's power, battery, alignment and gyroscopes are functioning. 'All missiles spinning, no defects.' Reeves puts on a combination headset, swings the microphone down and announces, 'All positions, WEO on the Net.'

In Sherwood Forest, Reeves' assistant has also put his headset on. With his team of ratings he executes the final checks, including balancing the pressure inside the missile tubes with the water pressure outside, so that the hatches can swing open freely. He ensures that nitrogen is used; it is an inert gas, which will not explode when the missiles are fired from the tubes.

In the control room, Southcott is listening into his headset. The announcement he has been awaiting from Reeves comes through. 'Captain, sir, weapon system in 1 SQ.' Mike Hawke acknowledges the report and says clearly, 'The Weapons Officer has my permission to fire.' He takes a red-painted key from where it always hangs on patrol – around his neck. He moves across to the overhead firing-board, inserts the key, and turns it.

In the MCC, a red panel-light printed with the words 'Captain's permission to fire' turns green. Reeves repeats, 'Captain's permission to fire. Roger.' Each missile will be fired separately, in a predetermined sequence. Within a few seconds another panel, displaying 'Missile prepared', switches from orange to green. The first hatch swings open. With a barely perceptible movement Reeves pulls the trigger.

It is extremely difficult to penetrate the bland armour of the naval officer who does not want to discuss the rights and wrongs of Polaris. They are of course highly trained, highly disciplined men who work alongside their apocalyptic weapons system every day. This easy familiarity with Armageddon helps them to accept the principle of the deterrent, but they are not such robots that they do not occasionally discuss it or dwell on it. On film, however, they will reveal very few of these thoughts.

Do they ever imagine, for instance, the possibility that one day the 'real thing' will happen? Mike Reeves, a mature and gentle man, considers his answer carefully.

'Yes, I think most of us do, from time to time. While we're actually in the process of the exercise we don't think about it because we're part of the mechanical side of the machine, and we look at it really as a straightforward engineering exercise to make sure that the machine works. We are all part of the machine, and that's I'm sure how it will be on the day. I do think about it at other times, but I don't think you should dwell on it too much. Obviously we've got something here that's quite dreadful, and it's unthinkable to use it, but at the end of the day that's what we're here to do and that's what we would do . . . I'm completely sold on deterrence, I have no doubts whatsoever. I think it works. I would be rather silly to be doing this job if I didn't think that.'

Mike Hawke will say even less. 'To carry the nation's deterrent is an exceedingly responsible job and must be taken terribly seriously. I would be very silly if I didn't believe in it, doing the job I'm doing now, but my own personal views of the morality or wisdom of the deterrent I'm afraid I keep personally to myself. I very seldom discuss it with anybody other than my immediate family.'

'Does it ever keep you awake on patrol, for instance?'

'No, not at all.'

'Not at all?'

'Not one moment.'

'It doesn't weigh on your mind?'

'No, it does not.'

Other officers, not just on this submarine, are prepared to discuss Polaris more deeply. Most display a genuine conviction that it is right for Britain to have the deterrent, but they do not always display a great deal of thought behind that conviction. Some have taken the trouble to work out likely political scenarios that could lead to the deterrent proving valuable; others feel that the sheer possession of it is sufficient to affect significantly the Soviet view of Britain and Europe. Very few, when pushed, could conceive of any Prime Minister authorising its use, except as an adjunct to American action. Some, worryingly, considered its most likely use would be as a 'warning shot', 'to show them we mean business'.

In many ways the most open comments came, not from the officers, but from the ratings. They acknowledge freely that they very seldom discuss the subject while they are on patrol, but suggest that this is not out of disinterest so much as an unwillingness to confront the reality of the situation.

'One of the reasons people don't talk about it is that we know it would be a last-ditch effort if we used them, and none of us would have anywhere to go back to. Really it's like cutting your own throat.'

'Nobody really thinks of ever having to use them. You just can't imagine it. There's never been a war like that before . . .'

'Still, I reckon that if a real firing signal came in they'd still go off all right – the reaction would set in afterwards.'

'Well, I think it's a pretty frightening thought, that you could surface four or five weeks later, and there's absolutely nothing left. We try not to think about it, but the reason we're doing this is to protect our families and friends at home – but when we've done our part, it's still done us no good because there'll be nothing left at home – it's a Catch-22.'

Of course, it is essentially unfair to expect deep and meaningful thoughts from all Polaris submariners any more than from the U-boat crews of the last two wars. They are there to do a job, and there is no reason why they should concern themselves a great deal with the politics of the weapons system that they happen to carry. It is always possible of course that the apparent paucity of considered views is actually the result of a subconscious need not to think about the situation that their job could ultimately lead them to.

However, as the government continues to commit itself to the constantly increasing cost of replacing the ageing Polaris with the new Trident system, I cannot help but think back for a moment to the Earl St Vincent, who 180 years ago was the first to realise that the submarine would be of the most use to the *weaker* naval power. Of course, he was thinking of direct conflict between submarine and surface warship, and had no inkling that the submarine's unique qualities would one day be used to threaten not just ships, but entire countries. Nevertheless, his philosophy can still be applied to Polaris, but at a higher level; for it is tempting to believe that Britain's investment in the submarine-based deterrent is the result of her declining influence in the world – nothing more than a relatively cheap way of buying apparent political influence.

HMS *Repulse*, unlike HMS *Warspite* and HMS *Oracle*, is of no direct value in the fighting defence of Britain. It is arguable whether it is of any value as a deterrent. The basic deterrence argument – that since both superpowers have so many nuclear weapons that neither could survive retaliation by the other, and therefore nuclear war will not happen – is a perfectly respectable one, although it does assume rationality in both Moscow and Washington.

The argument for a British independent deterrent is different. It says we must have nuclear capability so that, should we be forced into a situation where surrender to the advancing Russian forces seems the only option, then at least we can threaten to use our nuclear capability. But would not the Russians take a chance on that, since they could do so much more damage to our tiny island than we could do to them? After all, think how much damage they sustained in the last war, and the war before that, and in the fight against Napoleon.

Well, runs the pro-deterrent argument; they might sustain the damage – but they have no interest in an incinerated Britain, so they would hesitate to retaliate. Really? After the insult of receiving sixteen multi-headed Polaris missiles?

And then there's the argument that says we should not trust the Americans to protect Europe ad infinitum. Their increasing isolationism might ultimately tempt them to let Europe take care of itself, and refuse to risk a nuclear confrontation over a continent from which they are so far removed. If that situation arose, and we had no independent deterrent, we should be helpless – or, worse still, dependent on the French with their 'force de frappe'.

I'm afraid I find it impossible to believe that the Eagle would allow the Bear to swallow up all those priceless pots of honey, and in the process immeasurably strengthen its economy and resources, without action of some kind. The arguments can go on for ever. Even its staunchest allies would concede that the independent deterrent is a 'grey area'. There are no absolutes, no certainties, only speculations and beliefs. For me, coming into contact with the mechanics of the deterrent has served to crystallise my thoughts on it. Any deterrent, including the British independent deterrent, is only credible if there is a will to use it, *and if the other side believes that there is a will to use it*. Thus, to use a very crude analogy, if I am standing, with my family ranged alongside me, facing my enemy, I am unlikely to use my pistol against him if he is accompanied by a phalanx of hit-men with sub-machine-guns who will instantly massacre my family as well as me, the moment I fire. He knows that I am unlikely to commit my family to mass suicide, *and therefore he knows that I will not use my pistol*.

But then, of course, I might. . . .

Overleaf HMS *Repulse*. The numbers on the rudder are the height above the keel, so this steel iceberg stretches down the equivalent of a two-storey house into the water.

Index

Italic numerals refer to illustrations